GLORY, HALLELUJAH!

The Story
of the Campmeeting Spiritual

FROM NEW BEDFORD.

FROM NANTUCKET.

BATHING ON THE BEACH.

CAMP-MEETING AT MARTHA'S VINEYARD.

MARTHA'S VINEYARD is celebrated for its camp-meetings. Its location is peculiarly adapted to those who desire to mingle their holiday summer excursions with healthy spiritual enjoyment.

The *Tribune* correspondent thus describes the locality, and the means of reaching it:

between New Bedford and the Vineyard, and separating the Bay from the Sound.... A mile or thereabouts south of Holmes Hole, on the northeast shore of the island, is the grove in which the Wesleyan Methodists for many years past have been accustomed to hold one of the most remarkable camp-meetings in America. They first assembled here for prayer in 1835, and, except one brief interval, they have met here annually ever since, though it is only within the

owned by an association of Methodists, who have been offered a charter by the Massachusetts Legislature. There are over 200 cottages on the ground, one-fourth of which have been erected during the present summer. "In front," says the correspondent from whom we have already quoted, "there is a pretty little veranda, and three or four feet of garden may be fenced in before it. Over the front-door there is generally a balcony. The high-peaked roofs, the balconies,

tha's Vineyard at this season have more and fresher pleasures than those who summer at Newport or Long Branch. Here you see the latest fashions, and innocent flirtation is not unknown among the lads and lassies. They play croquet. Just below the steamboat landing there is a beach for bathing. And then there is fishing and sailing for those who are fond of aquatic sports, several good sail-boats being always at anchor off the pier. When evening sets in the girls put

THE PREACHERS' STAND.

"A sail of three hours takes you from the quaint little city of New Bedford, across Buzzard's Bay and Vineyard Sound, to Martha's Vineyard. If you must economize your time or money, or if there are ladies in your company, you will take the little steamboat which makes daily trips to the various towns along the Bay and Sound; but if there are no such overruling obstacles, a much better way will be to get a sail-boat at New Bedford and spend half a day on the excursion, cruising around the Elizabeth Islands, which lie

last six or seven years that their gatherings in this spot have acquired a national importance."

The daily attendance last year was 10,000; and this year it is probably greater, as not only New England but the Middle States contribute to the gathering. The camp is in a beautiful grove of scrub-oaks, washed on two sides by the sea, with a salt-water pond in its rear, into which the sea flows at high-tide over a narrow strip of beach. The grounds, including 150 acres, are

the door and window frames, are all decorated with scroll-work; stained glass, silver door-plates, hanging lanterns, and other luxuries are beheld at every turn; the houses are gayly painted, the verandas bloom with rare flowers, the little miniature yards are decked with moss and shell-work, and under the trees, which cast a thick shade over all, are rustic benches and swings for the children." Besides the cottages there are over 400 tents.

These thousands of people who frequent Mar-

away their croquet and attend to the tea-making; then comes the evening service around the cottage doors, while outside the gayly lighted streets of this improvised village. The utmost care is taken by the Committee of Regulations to prevent fire, and all smoking is forbidden in the tents.

Our artist, Mr. SHEPPARD, has seized upon some of the most picturesque features connected with this beautiful camp. The daily services began on the 24th of August.

COOKING.

SPECIMEN OF COTTAGES.

STYLE OF TENTS.

CAMP-MEETING, MARTHA'S VINEYARD—[SKETCHED BY W. L. SHEPPARD.]

GLORY, HALLELUJAH!

The Story
of the Campmeeting Spiritual

Ellen Jane Lorenz

ABINGDON
Nashville

GLORY, HALLELUJAH! THE STORY OF THE CAMPMEETING
SPIRITUAL

Library of Congress Cataloging in Publication Data

LORENZ, ELLEN JANE, 1907-
    Glory, hallelujah!

    Bibliography: p.
    Includes index.
    1.   Hymns, English—History and criticism.
2.   Revivals—Hymns—History and criticism.   3. Church
music—United States—History and criticism.   I.   Title.
ML3186.L86   783.6'7   79-24462

ISBN 0-687-14850-2

MANUFACTURED BY THE PARTHENON PRESS AT
NASHVILLE, TENNESSEE, UNITED STATES OF AMERICA

Contents

Preface

The walls of my study are lined with American hymnals from the nineteenth century. Most of them are rich in folk hymns, especially the rousing spirituals from the early nineteenth-century camp meetings. It was in these books that the present study found its inspiration and material. And these hymnals have a special meaning for me, because they were inherited from my grandfather, E. S. Lorenz. His name appears in a number of the books, not only as compiler and editor, but as composer and author—and occasionally in other compilers' prefaces, when acknowledgments of his help are noted. My study of his Collection has made me aware as never before of the part he played in the musical scene in the last quarter of the nineteenth century. I therefore bring the fruit of my studies to the public with a mixture of personal pride and excitement.

E. S. Lorenz (1854–1942) spent his entire life in the service of the church and its music. The son of a German immigrant, he began writing simple tunes when his father bought the small melodeon for which young Edmund had begged. While still in his teens, he was put to work by his denomination's publishing house (United Brethren, in Dayton, Ohio) compiling its first formal hymnal, *Hymns for the Sanctuary*. It and the many later hymnals and songbooks he compiled demonstrate his keen interest in American folk hymns. They also show his denomination's willingness to have those spirituals included in their official hymnals. His work as a compiler, and later as a publisher of church music, sparked his interest in hymns and hymnology, and he was to write several books about church music that stressed the importance of hymns.

Chapter 8 of his *Practical Church Music* (1909) is one of the earliest critical studies of the "American spiritual," as Lorenz called the folk hymns and campmeeting songs (perhaps the first time the term had been used for white spirituals). His discussion is not extensive, but it shows an awareness of the secular British source of many of the tunes, an awareness that is rare, if not unique, in the first decade of this century.

Several of E. S. Lorenz's hymnals and songbooks were used by pioneer folk hymnologist George Pullen Jackson as sourcebooks for folk hymns, and Jackson also acknowledged Lorenz's help in introducing him to *The Revivalist,* an 1868 treasury of most of the campmeeting songs of the North.[1] (See Section III b-2.) Appropriately, *The Revivalist* is the major ground from which my own study was harvested. The copy used was my grandfather's own; it bears a bookplate of Joseph Hillman, the compiler.

The E. S. Lorenz Collection offers, in addition, some Northern campmeeting songbooks not included in Jackson's or any other study of campmeeting spirituals of which I am aware.

This story of the camp meetings and their spirituals is based on a portion of my doctoral dissertation, "A Treasure of Campmeeting Spirituals," and on an address presented to the National Convocation of the Hymn Society of America in Winston-Salem, North Carolina, in April, 1978. A microfilm copy of the dissertation is available from University Microfilms International, Ann Arbor, Michigan (No. 79-16,965).

Some knowledge of the camp meetings and revivals themselves is basic to an understanding of the songs they produced. Since several writers have given full accounts of the Southern and the Pennsylvania Dutch camp meetings and their music, I have generally limited my discussion to the songs and songbooks of the Northern, English-language camp meetings and revivals.

I shall be telling you about the songs, about the way they developed and were sung, and about the persistence not only of the songs themselves, but of the rhapsodic spirit that inspired them then and continues to inspire similar expressions to the present day. I shall also be recounting some of the drama of the camp meetings, a drama unsurpassed in American history in its human emotions, ecstasy, and hysteria. The urban revivals of the Northeast also had their peculiar intensities. I tell about them often in the words of actual observers of the scene, with emphasis on the singing that took place there.

I have said above that the Lorenz Collection was the heart of the present study, but it could not satisfy all the demands. I visited and examined other collections, with enriching results. The following acknowledgments will indicate my debt to them and to persons who helped. Like all who write about America's folk hymns, I am grateful to George Pullen Jackson for his far-reaching pioneer work in the field. But my chief gratitude must be reserved for the spiritual legacy from my grandfather, E. S. Lorenz, to whose memory this book is dedicated.

Thanks to:

United Theological Seminary, Dayton, Ohio (United Brethren and Evangelical Collections);

Dayton Public Library (the Dayton Room);

American Antiquarian Society, Worcester, Massachusetts, where I was the recipient of a Fred Harris Daniels Fellowship;

Goshen College Library, Goshen, Indiana (the Hartzler Collection);

The Joint University Libraries (now the Vanderbilt University Library), Nashville, Tennessee (the George Pullen Jackson Papers);

Dargan-Carver Library, Nashville;

The United Methodist Library, Nashville;

The United Methodist Archives, Lake Junaluska, North Carolina;

James Rogers, Springfield, Illinois (Personal Collection of Hymnals);

The Library of Congress, Music Division;

GLORY, HALLELUJAH!

Leonard Ellinwood and Elizabeth Lockwood of the
Dictionary of American Hymnology Project;
Dr. Richard Crawford and Dr. William J. Reynolds, who
made valued suggestions;
Justina L. Showers (daughter of E. S. Lorenz) and James
B. Porter (my patient husband), who listened.

12

Part I.

Camp Meetings:
How They Began

Introduction

The campmeeting chorus has been described as the most American of all the American folk hymns.[1] Negro spirituals have their African flavor, the "white spirituals" their British origins. But the campmeeting choruses flowered spontaneously in the unplowed soil of the American frontier of 1800–1840.

They are hymns with tunes that can be *sung,* sung by the masses or the few, sung and enjoyed by the musically illiterate and the musically aware, alike. As we shall see, seldom has any kind of folk music been put to a more severe test of availability for *singing* than were the campmeeting spirituals. Even for today's often jaded musical appetites, campmeeting tunes and choruses make good singing.

With the recent upsurge of interest in Americana, in hymnology, and in folk music, campmeeting spirituals can take their place as a rewarding, informative, and entertaining source of part of one of America's most important cultural treasures. Today we may regard campmeeting spirituals with the curious eye of the hymn-lover or the antiquarian, intrigued with discovering a field of interest so thoroughly American, so important in the story of American music, and so disarmingly delightful. We may, if we wish, judge the songs impersonally and find much of significance and smile at their excesses. Or we may accept their joyous spirit in our own worship. We may join Don Yoder when he calls them the "spiritual arrows of God's grace."[2]

The chorus has become the hallmark of the campmeeting spirituals. Naïve, crude, ebullient, sometimes almost comic, the choruses seem to our sophisticated ears often lacking in beauty and reverence. Yet, when we understand the part they played in our early American hymnody and in the development of religious expression on our frontiers, we hear them with a new respect. This respect increases as we recognize the pervasiveness of the spirit that led to their creation. We become aware that the campmeeting spiritual and its choruses have an importance all their own.

The songs did have roots. Some of their characteristic forms are in the same patterns one finds in children's songs and the game-and-dance songs of older times. Other campmeeting choruses resemble the rhapsodic utterances of early religion in many lands. The word "hallelujah" was not invented in camp meetings!

For a long time the *music* was unpublished, transmitted only orally as preachers went from one camp meeting to another. The *words,* however, found a home almost at once, in little wordbooks, or "songsters," which sprang to life in each area where the campmeeting fever struck. We shall find out more about the songs, but to understand them, we must also know something about the camp meetings themselves, for it was there that the songs grew.

a. The First Camp Meetings

Camp meetings were a phenomenon of America's frontier in the very early nineteenth century. The frontier of the time was Kentucky, Tennessee, and southern Ohio. Soon it was pushed westward into Indiana, Illinois, southern Michigan, and Missouri, as well as southward.[3] The danger of Indians had been eased by the Treaty of Greenville (Ohio), 1795, but the many and constant dangers of the wilderness still remained. There were no schools, no established churches; settlements were far apart. Life was difficult—lonely, grim, uncertain.

Most of the pioneers were godless, rough people, who gambled and drank for their only recreation. But many of the frontierspeople had been sober, devout church members back in the East, and it was chiefly for their ministry that the eastern churches sent their missionary preachers to the frontier and established circuits in the wilderness that were covered by the itinerant preachers on horseback. The conversion of the Indians and the dissolute was of second priority. The autobiographies of some of these early circuit riders or itinerants—Cartwright, Fetterhof (see section c below), Finley, Young, *et al.*—give an excellent picture of the life of the times (see list of Recommended Reading, p. 139).

The first camp meetings were held in Kentucky in 1800, as the Second Great Awakening (see Section a of Part II) began to sweep the land. There had been earlier revivals: New England's First Great Awakening in the 1730s and 1740s,[4] and in the 1790s in North Carolina and elsewhere, but these had no actual camping on a large scale. The reason for the camping was that as attendance increased, the surrounding farmers could not provide victuals or lodging; hence the tents and campfires.

The idea of the camp meeting was instantly popular, for the frontierspeople were hungry for religion as well as for the sociability the meetings afforded. The meetings spread rapidly back to Virginia and the Carolinas, to Tennessee, across the Ohio River, and to the Northeast. As the frontiers were pushed west, the camp meetings went west also. Soon every state in the young country was holding camp meetings.

The meetings were frequently known by their location, and most of the names were waterways: Mud Creek, Turtle Creek, Red River, and the like.

The primary purpose of the meetings was to hold sacramental services, for the frontier had no churches to provide them, and the itinerant preachers visited but seldom. The solemn sacramental meetings climaxed the sessions, the one time when the noisy confusion was stilled and all could worship in comparative quiet.[5]

Rules were set up concerning behavior, living conditions, and schedule. Campmeeting manuals were published.

GLORY, HALLELUJAH!

b. Let's Go to a Camp Meeting! (1801)

But why should we read about the rules? Instead, let's go to a camp meeting and find out for ourselves. Suddenly you become a farmer in southwestern Ohio, in the very early years of the nineteenth century. You are a slave to the endless, backbreaking task of turning the wilderness into a home. Your nearest neighbor lives six miles downriver— but you have another kind of neighbor, *death,* which shadows you every minute of the day. Your wife and five children have no companionship outside the family; there are no schools, no churches. Back East, where you came from, you were a church-going Methodist, but here you are lucky if the itinerant preacher comes to your door three times a year on his four-hundred-mile circuit from the Scioto to the Miami. You miss going to church and receiving the sacraments; your Bible, the only book you have in your cabin, is read to tatters. It was the textbook from which your children learned to read.

Then one day in 1801, you hear from the circuit-rider preacher about some religious revivals down in Tennessee and Kentucky. Lately, you hear, these four- or five-day affairs have drawn so many people that there are not accommodations for them all. Now they are encouraged to bring tents and provisions for camping in the forest grove.

You decide to go. After all, the harvest is in, and Cane Ridge, Kentucky, is not far south of the Ohio River. So, following the waterways and trails and narrow roads, you travel to Cane Ridge. As you approach, you note that the countryside is virtually empty of inhabitants. Everyone seems to be headed for the camp on foot, by wagon, or by boat. You meet several persons who have walked twenty or thirty miles to the meeting. You are glad for your old wagon! You are awed by the beauty of the setting: the virgin forest, the clear rivers. As you finally arrive at the camp, you exclaim at the great clearing, edged by a half-circle of tents, wagons, and campfires. You look with pleasure at the fine grove, a place which, you are to learn later, had been recommended by Daniel Boone himself to

16

James McGready, the fiery preacher from North Carolina. That's the man, you remember hearing, who really started the idea of camp meetings in the wilderness.

You set up your tent with the others in the circle while your children gather wood for a big campfire. Then you walk around the camp. You see the tents around the edge of the clearing, and the torches and candles and campfires now illuminating the scene as night approaches.

You find out the rules: The trumpet signals for meetings or evening retirement. Separate lodging for men and women, a light always burning in the tents. The guarding of the camp by night watchmen. The prescribed family prayers, the singing and praying during intermissions, the times for exhortation and religious conversations, the four preaching services.[6]

The rule that pleases you the most is one that tells you you may sing as much as you please: "It shall be in order, when public services are not being held, to pray and sing and shout as much as you please, and as loud as you please (Hallelujah!), only do not unduly protract your devotions."[7]

You notice the benches, those on one side for the women, on the other for the men. You walk around the camp, examining the stands erected for the preachers, with space only for a Bible and a hymnbook. You see several of the stands, for there are far too many people to be served by one preaching—thousands of people. Someone tells you there are twenty thousand, another says thirty! You hear a man say Kentucky is getting too crowded these days with its 220,000 people. You think people must be hungry for religion: some came from farther away than you did—two hundred miles and more.

You are excited now by the crowd and the singing and the preaching and the shouting. What a noise the people are making! You can scarcely hear the preachers, for everyone is singing or shouting. Over there are about a dozen circles of people, each circle singing a different hymn. You join one of the circles and sing several hymns by Wesley or Hart.

The place seems continually vocal with psalms, hymns, and spiritual songs, alternating with prayer.[8]

Near the stands in front are men exhorting sinners to seek salvation or suffer eternal damnation. Look! one of the exhorters is a woman! Can you believe that? You admit she is a good shouter, but, really, she ought to save her talking and singing and praying for a woman's group, not a promiscuous gathering like this. You say this to one of the preachers, and do you know what he answers? He says:

> You think women are proper teachers for our schools, and every circle of our society except religion. God employed a dumb ass to rebuke the prophet, and a dunghill fowl to send conviction to the heart of backslidden Peter; and I see no reason why a woman should not reprove sin. . . . You and your creed belong to a bygone age, when a woman scarcely dared speak in the presence of her husband, and silence and inaction were enjoined on account of her (supposed) inferiority. That day has passed. Woman has been redeemed by the blood of Christ and exalted to equality with man in the privileges and blessings of the Gospel dispensation.[9]

Then you wonder about the Negroes. Is it customary to have them pitch their tents next to those of the whites? And sing and exhort and even preach together with us? But your preacher friend tells you that everyone is welcome, and that there are many good Christians among the Negroes who will no doubt get to heaven.[10] You suddenly feel good about this, for it's obvious that they are the life of the camp meeting, and their preachers are good ones. You like to hear them singing; they have melodious voices and it seems that the more they sing the better they get.[11] The man in the tent next to yours tells you that Indians also come to camp meetings and are good singers, too.

But the thing that disturbs you most is that *children* are encouraged to preach and exhort. You stand in wonder as a ten-year-old quotes Scripture in a way that puts your children's knowledge of the Bible to shame.[12] But you frown at your own when they show signs of speaking in public. It is not good for the young ones to be made so much over.

You have already noticed that there are preachers from several different denominations—Methodist, Baptist, Presbyterian, even Shaker. You decide that the best part of the camp meeting, after the singing, is the welcome to *everyone,* no matter what age, sex, race, or denomination. That's the way America ought to be, you think.

Now the Methodist preacher is lining out a hymn, and you hurry over to join in the singing. There are no hymnbooks except on the preachers' stands, but many of the people know some hymns of Watts and Wesley by heart. You sing along, as loud as you can. Bishop Asbury would have approved of this "holy noise,"[13] and you do, too. You agree with the preacher who said that among the common people volume is an element of power in praising God. A hymn must have *capacity!*[14]

What a giant sound! The very forest seems alive with the great volume of the singing! And then the shouting that follows! Everyone bellowing out *Hallelujah!* or *Amen!* or *Glory to God!* all at once, and the Methodists clapping in time to the music! Some fall on their knees and pray aloud. The confusion is beyond belief. It's as if a wave of—what shall you call it, *ecstasy?*—has swept over everyone. Yes, you've heard it called the "singing ecstasy," and also "wildfire."[15] You go out of your head with excitement and yell with the rest of them. And you sing—oh, how you sing![16]

But look over there! What is happening? People are falling down as if in a trance, hundreds of them. The preacher seems excited about them and calls them the "slain of the Lord." This falling looks to you as if a gigantic sword, unseen, were striking an army, row after row.

You wonder what causes this peculiar falling, and you decide it is the intensity of emotion wrought by the powerful exhortations and the preaching. Someone tells you that more than a thousand are "slain" at a time! Imagine!

Other seizures are even stranger: the "holy laugh," leaping, dancing, rolling. Over there a woman's head is jerking back and forth; she tries to control it, but can't. Her hair is snapping back and forth like a whip. You have little sympathy for the "barking exercise," in which men stand under a tree and bark like dogs, thinking they have treed the devil.

But one exercise is really beautiful: the "holy singing." This singing issues not from the mouth or the nose, but from the breast, in a curious way, and it sounds like a choir of the angelic host.

You note that those who succumb to the exercises are not just the young, the unstable, or even the most religious, but also some dignified citizens, some preachers (that really surprises you!), and even some skeptics. You see one of the jeering onlookers who surround the camp suddenly start to jerk his head back and forth, like the woman. He tries to stop it, bewildered, but his whole body is convulsed with jerking. Finally he runs away into the woods, twitching all over. You can scarcely believe such a thing could happen.

Of course, you and your fellow frontiersmen are accustomed to rough behavior and know how to cope with rowdies. You've heard tell that sometimes the preachers have bodily pitched pretenders from the camp meetings. Will that happen here?

Now you force your attention away from these antics and join again in the singing. There is singing going on at every hour of the day and night. The sound of that throng raising their voices in the forest temple, thousands upon thousands of voices, is something you'll never forget. As the holy song rises and floats out on the stillness of the night, you feel that surely this place is holy ground.[17]

Later, when you are asked about the songs, who wrote them and how the congregation learned them, you are perplexed for an answer. "We had no hymnbooks there," you say. "The preachers each had one, and they led us. Some of the hymns I had learned back East. But as for the choruses, they just seemed to come to us as a gift from the

Holy Spirit.'' Of course, the preachers may have something
to do with it. How they sing, and how we praise God for
their good singing![18]

You have often heard your own itinerant preacher
singing as he rode along the wilderness trail on his horse.
When he stopped at your cabin for the night, he sang from
his hymnbook almost as much as he read from the Bible and
prayed. He has a good voice, and therefore is assured a
double welcome and a double harvest of souls.[19]

Here at camp last night you saw a funny thing happen
when Brother Warren sang a hymn in a nearby tent. A
wonderful influence seemed to come instantly upon all
present. An old lady forgot she was cooking supper and in
her excitement and joy threw her arms up, still holding on
to the frying pan handle, and scattered the ham and gravy
around the tent. There stood the old lady, apparently
unable to move, holding up that huge frying pan in an
attitude that reminded one of Jupiter about to hurl a
thunderbolt. It was a great time, but we lost a good supper
of ham and eggs![20]

It is time to take your leave of Cane Ridge. You and your
family know sorrow at the thought of leaving this place of
spiritual nourishment where you have made new friends.
Now you must start toward home, and you are engulfed
already in the thought of the loneliness that awaits you
there. The final trumpets are sounded, and with the others
you sing the doxology, form a procession, and two by two
follow the ministers as they march, singing, three times
around the camp. It is a touching scene, and, though you
try, you can't hide your tears.

You will never forget the parting songs that were sung as
you walked in that procession, for you and your family sing
them over and over again as you travel back to Ohio. (See
Songs 2 through 5 in Part V.)

After your return, you begin to wonder. Are the
frenzies, the hysteria, and the wild behavior obscuring the
real purpose and achievement of the camp meetings? The

21

next time the itinerant preacher visits, you ask him if he thinks the camp meetings are worthwhile. He answers:

Yes, they are surely the work of the Lord. You are worried about the pretenders, the backsliders? We have them here, and at camp meetings, yes, and everywhere. You are distressed about the falling and the confusion? This kind of thing has attended religious awakening since the beginning of Christianity, though perhaps not in such great numbers. Have you read about the Wesley meetings? The Jonathan Edwards meetings in Connecticut sixty years ago? . . . What about what happened at Pentecost?

We Methodist preachers as a rule don't encourage the exercises. I've heard Bishop Asbury preach against them, and I'm told that John Wesley never condoned using tricks to gain converts. . . . Much may be said about the camp meetings, but take them all in all, for unfeigned and fervent spirituality, give me a country camp meeting against the world! [21]

c. Camp Meetings Become Established

Now we say good-bye to our singing farmer from Ohio. After the Kentucky beginnings, the campmeeting excitement spread quickly in all directions, accompanied by its new songs. In 1811 there were four hundred camp meetings; by 1820 almost a thousand had been held.[22] The accompanying growth of the churches, especially the Methodist, was the ultimate tribute to the success of the camp meetings.

To understand what was going on in the frontiers of the first half of the nineteenth century, let's make the acquaintance of two of the itinerant preachers who, as it happened, wrote their memoirs. The first one was perhaps the most famous of all the Methodist circuit riders, Peter Cartwright; the second was unknown beyond his small denomination—John Fetterhof, a United Brethren preacher who came to Ohio from the Pennsylvania Dutch country.

Peter Cartwright was a character. He had a sense of humor rather like that of Will Rogers, and he was as homespun and as widely loved as that later gentleman. Born in 1785 in Virginia, he moved as a boy to the roughest, wildest part of the Kentucky frontier, Logan County. His father taught him how to handle himself in times of danger, and Peter was known far and wide for his ability to subdue ruffians who threatened the peace of the camp meetings. He would avoid a fight as long as possible, but when the time came, he could use his fists well. "It was part of my creed to love everybody but to fear no one," he said. He also could use his wits, and enjoyed recounting tales of his triumphs in his memoirs. There was, for instance, the story of a group of young scoffers, who, as they rode home ahead of Cartwright after a meeting in 1829, pretended to be new converts, singing campmeeting songs lustily. Presently their carriage overturned in a mud hole. Cartwright drew up behind them and mimicked their singing: "Glory, hallelujah! Another sinner down!"[23]

Converted at age seventeen, he was at once appointed to exhort the wicked, and within a year set about organizing a new circuit in this rough area. He had hoped to go to school, but he had to school himself on his own, as he traveled the circuit. He became an avid reader and a skillful preacher, and knew his Bible and his hymnbook from cover to cover.

His book gives a vivid picture of the hard life of an itinerant, a job that he kept up for over sixty years. He spent several months a year at the campgrounds; he was converted on a campground, and the most successful part of his ministry was in camp meetings.

He had a good strong voice; he could speak and sing and exhort all the day and night long for the week of the camp meeting. He knew the language of the people to whom he preached and could move them to tears or ecstasy or to terror of their sinful state. His account of his life contains hundreds of times the sentence "I sung a hymn and preached and prayed." He spoke out boldly, not only against sin but also against doctrines and customs he did not approve of: Baptist immersion, Unitarianism, Calvinism, seminary-trained young preachers, church choirs and organs, cushioned pews, fancy clothes. In Boston in 1852 for a conference, he said to a local preacher:

There's your old wooden god, the organ, bellowing up in the gallery, and a few dandified singers lead in the singing, and really do it all. The congregation won't sing, and when you pray, they sit instead of kneeling. We don't worship God in the west by proxy or substitution.[24]

Forty-five years of his service were spent in Illinois, where he was a state representative. He ran for Congress, but was defeated by Abraham Lincoln. Although a friend of the Negro, he opposed the tactics of the extreme abolitionists.

To know this virile, honest, energetic man, eccentric but sincere, one must read his own engaging story.

John Fetterhof was in some ways Cartwright's opposite. Mild, self-effacing, he still was an effective and popular preacher who was not afraid to speak out his disdain for the new-fashioned acceptance of relaxed standards. Born in 1798 in Pennsylvania, he was a bilingual preacher, with German as his native tongue. After his conversion he was sent to Ohio, where he preached and traveled until he died at eighty-four. His yearly income seldom exceeded thirty dollars, but by his own effort he provided himself with a house and a farm. Like Cartwright, he had a good voice and could lead the singing. The unique experiences of John Fetterhof were his frequent preaching for the blacks, whom he enjoyed and admired, his admiration of women in the pulpit, and his intimate association with the Methodists, for whom also he often preached.[25]

Here are two excerpts from Fetterhof's story (which is far less spritely than that of the feisty Cartwright).

Heard Lydia Sexton preach. . . . She is a warmhearted speaker, and a good revivalist. She has traveled extensively, and has held many protracted meetings, and nearly all of them a great success. . . .

This month I preached much for the colored Baptists. We always had much of the power of God with us. They are an honest, upright people. . . . There was much shouting and noise among them. When they get happy they call it being "fired up."[26]

As the old frontier became settled, and churches with "located" preachers were established, the religious and social needs of the people were satisfied in their own neighborhood, and the need for camp meetings lessened. By the 1840s, they had virtually disappeared in the South.[27] In the North, however, stimulated by the Holiness movement, there was considerable campmeeting activity until several decades after the Civil War. By 1870 the facilities of the campgrounds had been made permanent, with an auditorium or at least a roofed shed, water systems, cottages, and other civilized comforts. By then the meetings emphasized even more strongly the renewal of the already converted as against the salvation of sinners. Eventually, most of the campgrounds turned into Chautauquas, with concerts, classes, plays, and lectures.

In Pennsylvania and the "West" (Ohio was the West in those early days), German-speaking churches such as the Evangelical and the United Brethren continued the use of the camp meeting and sang its songs until the end of the century, even into the twentieth. Other organizations to continue the tradition were the Wesleyan Methodists, the Nazarenes, the Church of God, and the Salvation Army. Some denominations, such as the Southern Baptists and the Christian Missionary Alliance, still hold old-fashioned camp meetings every summer. But they have nothing quite like the old-time ecstasies.

d. What People Said About the Early Camp Meetings (Nineteenth-Century Commentary)

The fame of the early camp meetings spread all over the country. Newspapers, church periodicals, pamphlets, and books carried articles about the meetings or notices of forthcoming ones. The clergy of the more sedate denominations wrote diatribes against the camp meetings; the clergy of the participating denominations wrote spirited defenses, glowing accounts, in the high-flown language of the times. Most of these comments make us smile today, but the meetings were a favorite topic for many decades. Some of the comments are reprinted here.

People Talked About the Gathering Crowds

During the progress of the meetings, immense crowds were seen in all directions, passing and repassing upon the roads and paths, while the woods adjacent to the meetings seemed to be alive with people. Whole communities and sections of the country appeared to be depopulated . . . and all ages, sexes, and conditions were pressing on to the great camp meeting. (Isaac Smucker, "The Great Awakening," *Proceedings of the American Antiquarian Society at the Annual Meeting in Boston, April 29, 1874* [Worcester: Charles Hamilton, 1874], p. 62.)

It would seem proper that persons traveling a distance to, and from Camp-meeting, should beguile the tediousness of the way, by singing Hymns comporting with their views and feelings on the way. (Enoch Mudge, *American Camp Meeting Hymn Book,* 1818, Preface.)

People Exclaimed over the Beautiful Setting

There is a peculiar charm about camp meetings. We worship in God's great cathedral, in nature's magnificent temple, arched over with the brilliant heavens, and floored with the beautiful green earth— under the foliage of trees planted by God's own hand. There is a kind of grandeur about such a temple that accords with man's noble origin and lofty destiny. (A. P. Mead, *Manna in the Wilderness,* [Philadelphia: Perkenpine & Higgins, 1860], p. 6.)

Few can look upon a camp meeting scene and not be moved. . . . The sound of the trumpet, and the gathering together of thousands, who pass to and fro with lights and torches, all has a tendency to awaken the most solemn reflections. And when the holy song rises from a thousand voices, and floats out upon the stillness of the night air, the listener must feel that surely such a place is holy ground. (James B. Finley, *Autobiography; or Pioneer Life in the West,* ed. W. P. Strickland [Cincinnati: Methodist Book Concern, 1854], p. 345.)

People Commented on the Activities and the Confusion

In the time of preaching, if care is taken, there is but little confusion; when that is over, and the singing, and praying, and exhortation begin, the audience is thrown into what I call real disorder. The careless fall down, cry out, tremble, and not infrequently are affected with convulsive twitchings. Among these the pious are very busy, singing, praying, conversing, falling down in extacies, fainting with joy, exhorting sinners, combating opposers, etc. . . . Then . . . the shout is raised Glory be to God for a new born soul. And the holy embrace follows. . . . Nothing that imagination can paint, can make a stronger impression on the mind, than one of those scenes. Sinners dropping down on every hand, shrieking, falling down in distress for sinners or in raptures of joy! Some singing, some shouting, clapping their hands, hugging and even kissing, laughing; others talking to the distressed, to one another, or to opposers of the work, and all this at once.—No spectacle can inspire a stronger sensation. And with what is doing, the darkness of the night, the solemnity of the place, and of the occasions, and the conscious guilt, all conspire to make terror thrill through every power of the soul, and rouse it to awful attention. (Letter from Moses Hoge to Ashbel Green, in William W. Woodward, *Surprising Accounts of the Revival of Religion* [Philadelphia: William Woodward, 1802].)

After sermon, a prayer-meeting was held in front of the stage, which a bedlam of bedlams would be nothing compared to it—Some singing, some praying, some jumping, some clapping and wringing their hands: one falling here, another there, crying, "Glory to God, I am happy; the Lord has entered me"—then bursting forth in another place and singing—

> Shout, shout, we are gaining ground;
> Glory, Halleluiah!
> Satan's kingdom, 'twill come down;
> Glory, Halleluiah!

Another crying out, "We will pray old Satan's kingdom down—Blessed be God, brother, Satan can't stand here." (*A Treatise on the Proceedings of a Camp Meeting Held in Bern, N.Y., County of Albany* [Albany: Webster and Skinner, 1810], p. 9.)

People Were Enthralled by the Singing

The music of the camp meeting! who, that has ever heard it, has not paused to drink the rich melody into his soul? It comes with a grandeur, a softness and sweetness, that can be heard nowhere else. In the measured strains of a multitude of voices, uttered in charming melody, and unbroken by walls, it swells in solemn grandeur and rolls deliciously through the forests, awaking re-echoing cadences on every hand. (Mead, *Manna*, p. 142.)

Songs and hymns were sung and shouts were fairly howled to a degree only limited by the utmost powers of the human voice. (C. W. Christman, Jr., *Camp Meetings in the York Annual Conference*, pamphlet [1849], p. 4.)

I hear a noise in their camp, . . . the noise of them that sing, do I hear. . . . Their felicity exceeds my expectations. . . . A serenade of music cheered all their spirits, which never desisted from their first coalition until they decamped, and everyone sung what they pleased, and to the tunes with which he was best acquainted; under the sound of this general melody there was a band of preachers . . . & they with animation, and with powerful vociferation harangued as many as could hear consistent with the melody. (Adam Rankin, *A Review of the Noted Revival in Kentucky, 1801* [Lexington: John Bradford, 1802], p. 16.)

The preachers came down from their stand, and placed themselves in the midst of it, beginning to sing a hymn, calling upon the penitents to come forth. As they sang they kept turning themselves round to every part of the crowd, and, by degrees, the voices of the whole multitude joined in chorus. This was the only moment at which I perceived any thing like the solemn and beautiful effect which I had heard ascribed to this woodland worship. It is certain that the combined voices of such a multitude heard at dead of night, from the depths of their eternal forests, the many fair young faces turned upward, and looking paler and lovelier as they met the moonbeams, the dark figures of the officials in the middle of the circle, the lurid glare thrown by the altar-fires on the woods beyond, did altogether produce a fine and solemn effect, that I shall not easily forget. (Frances Trollope, *Domestic Manners of the Americans,* 1832; reprinted from the 5th ed., 1839 [New York: Dodd, Mead, 1927], p. 142.)

At the commencement of the revival, those familiar hymns, known in all our orthodox congregations, were used, but it was soon felt that they gave but imperfect expression to the ardent feelings of the worshippers.

The deficiency here was principally supplied by the preachers. (B. St. James Fry, "The Early Camp Meeting Song Writers," *The Methodist (Quarterly) Review,* July, 1859, p. 407.)

In the days of the great preachers "it appeared that the world would be converted through the instrumentality of the campmeeting song." (Jacob Young, *Autobiography of a Pioneer* [Cincinnati: L. Swormstedt and Poe, for the Methodist Episcopal Church, 1859], p. 524.)

People Were Impressed by the Farewell Service

After the Doxology was sung . . . a procession was formed, the ministers walking arm in arm followed by a great multitude, male and female, singing of the Lamb. They encompassed the camp circle three times, then they moved on . . . in perfect peace and good will to each other. (A. McLean and J. W. Eaton, *Penuel, or Face to Face with God* [New York: W. C. Palmer, Jr., Publisher, 1869], p. 482.)

After a very fervent prayer and the accustomed benediction, the parting scene succeeded which was truly affecting. The preachers first shook hands on the stands. The people crowded by scores and hundreds, their hands extended, their eyes glistening with tears, and their bosoms heaving with big emotion. After a most affectionate farewell, . . . they reluctantly struck their tents and dispersed from the place. (Francis Ward, *Minutes of a Camp Meeting Held by the Methodists in the Town of Carmel, Dutchess Co., 1804,* pamphlet [New York: John C. Totten, 1804], p. 7.)

People Approved of the Welcome to All

If now be [anyone] stood in the present light and felt his heart glow with love to the souls of men, he was welcome to sing, pray, or call sinners to repentance.

Neither was there any distinction as to age, color, or anything of a temporal nature: old and young, male and female, black and white had equal privilege to minister the light which they received. (Richard McNemar, *The Kentucky Revival, or, a Short History of the Late Extraordinary Outpouring of the Spirit of God in the Western States of America* [Reprinted by E. O. Jenkins, New York, 1846; Cincinnati, 1807], pp. 30-31.)

(In 1842 G. W. Henry attended a camp meeting in Maryland where five hundred white and about five hundred colored persons attended. The latter had tents in half-circles by themselves. Sometimes a black preacher held forth. Blacks and whites mingled in the evening.)

The blacks were the life of the camp meeting. Nine out of ten of them would have a melodious voice for singing and praying and shouting, at a great distance from the campground. (G. W. Henry, *Trials and Triumphs in the Life of G. W. Henry* [Oneida: G. W. Henry, 1853, 1856], p. 269.)

Soon the Christian chiefs and queens and all were formed in a circle, and the voice of praise and prayer made the forest arches ring. After singing one of their Christian songs, as only Indians can sing, they fell on their knees and lifted up their faces toward heaven as if they expected the Great Spirit to descend. (James B. Finley, *Sketches of Western Methodism* [Cincinnati: Methodist Book Concern, 1856], p. 518.)

A little girl was brought into the ring crying; they told her she must pray to the Lord for the power of the Spirit, or she would go to hell. (*A Treatise on the Proceedings of a Camp Meeting,* 1810, p. 5.)

Nature itself may be said to teach us that woman cannot quit her sphere of relative subordination with regard to man without dishonoring herself and losing her proper strength. . . .[The camp meeting] encourages women to pray in public, and to address promiscuous meetings, and, by the spirit it infuses, makes them willing to unsex themselves in this way. (John W. Nevin, *The Anxious Bench,* 3rd ed. [Reading, Pa.: Daniel Miller, Publisher, 1892; originally published, 1843]; p. 101.)

. . . Heard Amanda Smith, a colored woman. She is a mystery to all who hear her. She has a well-balanced mind, warm with the love of God, and well seasoned with grace, and her singing is rapturous; it carries the mind away. (Fetterhof, *Life of John Fetterhof,* 1883, p. 240.)

People Were Amazed at the Ecumenicity

In this glorious work, the Methodist and Baptist ministers and people heartily united at this early period . . . and mutually agreed with the Presbyterian brethren to drop all disputes about non-essentials, and as the heart of one man, in the unity of the spirit and in the bond of peace, to use their utmost exertions for promoting the cause of God among the people. (Preface to *A Collection of the Most Admired Hymns and Spiritual Songs,* 1815.)

Some, perhaps, will censure us for associating with the Baptists and the Methodists: But, my dear sir, we are all very friendly; there appears to be good doing; all are encouraging it. . . . We all preach the truth, as we think, carefully observing decorum, as far as conscience will admit, that one society may not hurt the feelings of another. (William W. Woodard, *Surprising Accounts of the Revival of Religion,* 1802.)

All congregational assemblies are swallowed up in this multitude: no man preaches in his own pulpit; the whole have happily united in one congregation, and move like the lovely hosts of Israel. They all eat and drink at one table, and all lie in one bed; they possess all the pleasures of social fellowship. (Adam Rankin, *A Review of the Noted Revival in Kentucky, 1801, p. 15.*)

People Championed the Meetings' Effectiveness

But not withstanding all the honest demur of good people, and the malignant hostility of the wicked, . . . the salutary effects of these meetings have been most triumphantly demonstrated. Thousands upon thousands have been truly regenerated, whilst many tens of thousands have experienced the quickening and sanctifying power of divine grace. (Frederick Plummer, *Diary, 1787–1854,* manuscript [Worcester: American Antiquarian Society, 1854], p. 186.)

e. What Was Happening in the Eastern Cities

After their Kentucky beginnings, the country camp meetings spread quickly in all four directions. At the same time, the Second Great Awakening had also affected the urban population, but in a somewhat different way. The results of the revivals held so successfully by Jonathan Edwards during the First Great Awakening (1734 and after) had evaporated; the country was preoccupied with the material aftermath of the Revolution. It was time for renewed religious aggression.

The new revivals in the Northeast (1798–1840) differed from the camp meetings in that they were held in a church or other auditorium, and they were dominated by a revivalist on whose leadership the success of the revival depended. What's more, the meetings were sober in contrast to the flamboyance of the early camp meetings— even though the revivalists freely played on the emotions.

Unlike the frontier revivalists, most of the city preachers were well educated: only two of thirty-six prominent Presbyterian leaders were not college graduates.[28] But

Methodist urban preachers tended to be handicapped by
their lack of education, although such a handicap had been
considered an advantage on the frontier.[29]

In the end, of course, one uses the long-term increase in
church membership as a measuring stick of the revivals'
success. The gain was indeed large, but some of it was soon
dissipated by the attraction of new movements, both
religious and moral, which took hold of the area. Especially
in up-state New York, where revivalist Charles G. Finney's
major work had been, people turned to Mormonism,
Spiritualism, Millennialism (see Part III b-5), social
reforms, and communal living with just as much fervor as
they had shown for revival meetings.[30] Indeed, even the
revivalists were "actively engaged in the front ranks of the
various reform drives."[31]

In 1858 there was another wave of powerful revivals.
These were occasioned by the Panic of 1857, when
businessmen, their firms in hard straits, gathered in weekday
prayer meetings that united men of all denominations. This
was an era of lay activity.[32] Some of the most important
books of revival spirituals were published as the result of this
religious activity. After that, and even during that, the gospel
song was rising swiftly. (See Part IV b.)

Revival meetings have continued to the present time;
each decade has had its master revivalist, and music still
plays an important part in stirring the emotions.

f. Recollections of a Fictitious
Revival Enthusiast (1870)

(To taste the flavor of the city revivals in the Northeast,
let's interview a *fictitious* old-time resident of Troy, New
York, which was a center of revivalism during most of the
first three-quarters of the nineteenth century. The year is
1870, and Amanda North is about fifty-five years old.)

Amanda North, that's my name, and if you are interested
in revivals of religion in these parts, you've come to the

right person, I guess, for I've been attending revivals ever since I was a youngster over in Oneida, nearly forty-five years ago. My folks were Presbyterians, but I've been a Methodist since I first moved to Troy, as a bride.

Charles Finney? Of course I know about Charles Grandison Finney. My mother took me to one of his revival meetings when I was about ten, in Oneida. She claimed he was the best preacher New York State ever produced. But he scared me half to death when I went to that meeting, back in '26, I guess it was.

Why? It was his eyes, for one thing. They followed me. Seemed no matter where that man stood he was always staring at me with those burning eyes of his. Except when he was praying in the pitch-dark prayer room. That scared me even more. Him on his knees, praying, calling people by name for their sins, and folks sobbing and moaning. I began to cry, and mother took me home, and I didn't go to any revival meetings for a while. My father wouldn't stand for it. No place for a child, he said—though later he did let me go to one of Rev. Edward Hammond's special revivals for children. I remember confessing my sins to *him*. Jealous of my pretty sister, I think that was my worst one. I thought I was surely going to hell. But Mr. Hammond was gentle, not like Mr. Finney.

My mother well-nigh worshiped that man. She went to every meeting of his that she could get to. She helped him: organized the women's prayer group, called on the new converts, and such.

No, you're right—there wasn't much singing at Mr. Finney's revival meetings. Mother said that when she begged him for more singing, he told her that he had never known of a singing revival which amounted to much. It was prayer, prayer, and more prayer that made revivals succeed, he said.[33] Mother used to declare that old Mr. Nash, Mr. Finney's assistant, could pray a horse from one pasture to another.[34] Mr. Finney let mother pray in public at some of his meetings, but lots of the church folks thought it was contrary to Bible teaching to let a woman be that bold in public. Some other churches even let women *preach* in public, but never the Presbyterians. Later on, Mr. Finney was severely criticized by other preachers for letting women pray at his meetings.[35] But he didn't let that faze him; he knew what he wanted, and no man could change his mind for him. Mr. Finney came to Troy for over a month a few years back. I went to some of his meetings, and he still knew how to cast a spell on everyone, even us Methodists—but I missed the singing.

In those days all the denominations joined in putting on revival meetings—the Baptists, the Episcopalians, the Methodists, and the Presbyterians. After all, everyone was expecting the end of the world to come soon, and on Judgment Day all would be judged alike.[36] So they worked together like one big family during the revival. But after the meetings were over and the revivalists had left town, you should have heard the squabbling about which church should get which converts! It was a real fight. Unchristian, my father called it.

When I moved to Troy, I joined the Methodist Church because Methodists sang a lot, and I loved to sing hymns. Not those old Yankee psalm-tunes. They're too slow, but the lively ones from the West. That's the kind of music I like to sing at a revival meeting. I think it helps people, to sing those shouting choruses. It's—well, it's like a safety valve after one of those long sermons that get a person all roused up.[37]

There was always a revival meeting going on in Troy, it seemed. I remember old Mr. Nettleton, from the East—he frowned on the campmeeting songs. Lyman Beecher came to Troy, too. Nathaniel Beman was the preacher at Troy's Presbyterian Church, and when he led a revival meeting he imitated Mr. Finney's style, staring and shouting and calling on people by name. The one I liked best, though, was a Methodist, Rev. John Maffitt, back in '44, or '45, who let us sing all those hallelujah choruses from the Kentucky camp meetings.

Most of the songs we sang are in Mr. Hillman's new

book. Do you know that book? *The Revivalist.* Wait, I'll show you my copy; it was published just two years ago, in '68. The Methodists have published an astonishing lot of revival songbooks—even though the bishops don't approve.[38] Mr. Hillman's is one of the best. Have you ever heard of Mr. Joseph Hillman? He's not a preacher, he's a businessman in Troy. Insurance, I think. He's really devoted to his church—Sunday-school superintendent, leader of the Troy Praying Band—you know, they go all over the state and help revivalists put on meetings. And he's the man who organized our beautiful campground at Round Lake, near here. If you've never been to a Round Lake camp meeting, you've missed something grand. The singing there, it's what I expect heaven to sound like! . . .

g. What People Said About the City Revivals
(Nineteenth-Century Commentary)

People Talked About Their Effect

Bristol [R.I.] is a gay and prosperous town, an unusually wicked slave trade center. The Episcopalians, Congregationalists, Baptists, and Methodists all at once experienced the Spirit of the Lord as to baffle description. The town was paralyzed and business was suspended. All ages were concerned for a better world. On everyone's tongue was, not "What's the news?" but "What shall we do to be saved?" Rooms of carnal amusement were used for prayer. Fishermen abandoned their boats and spent the day in prayer. "What hath God wrought!" (William Rogers, *A Brief Account of the Late Wonderful Work of God at Bristol, R.I.* [Newburyport: W. and J. Gilman, 1812], pamphlet.)

It is now a most solemn time in this city. Let a stranger enter any congregation within this metropolis . . . and he will see more than usual attention and anxiety among them to know the things of the Kingdom of heaven. (Joshua Bradley, *Accounts of Religious Revivals in Many Parts of the United States from 1815–1818* [Albany: G. J. Loomis and Company, 1818], p. 232.)

On Sunday Bro. Spicer preached on the last judgment, and such power attended the word that very many fell from their seats screaming for mercy; others became so affrighted as to run, and Spicer cried after them, "Run, run, for the devil is after you!" (John Fetterhof, *Life of John Fetterhof of the United Brethren in Christ*, p. 76.)

People Reported on Children's Part in Revivals

Mr. Hammond's first meeting was for children, one of great power. At the close of his address, hundreds of children, among them two of his own, remained at the meeting, many weeping for their sins. (Edward Payson Hammond, *The Harvest Work of the Holy Spirit*, ed. P. C. Headley [Boston: Henry Hoyt, 1863], p. 297.)

People Discussed Singing in Revivals

Singing during a revival is an important part of religious exercise. . . . An appropriate verse, well sung, at the right time, will sometimes do more to assist the struggling spirit to take hold on Christ by faith, than a long sermon or a long prayer. (Luther Lee, *The Revival Manual* [New York: Wesleyan Methodist Book Room, 1850].)

I would urge all who desire to promote revivals of religion . . . to have the best singing you can in all your meetings. Sing with life and spirit. God appointed singing, and will bless it. (William C. Conant, *Narratives of Remarkable Conversions and Revival*

Incidents [New York: Derby and Jackson, 1858], p. 28.)

Then they sing hymns, pray, exhort, sing and pray again, till the excitement reaches a very high pitch indeed. (Frances Trollope, *Domestic Manners of the Americans,* 1832, p. 63.)

The singing of appropriate hymns performs a very important part in promoting revivals. I believe that there is as much conviction lodged in the mind by singing as by preaching. The melody softens the feelings, and the sentiment of the hymns leaves its stamp upon the melting heart and ripens into fruit. [!] The singing keeps the people together more than the preaching. The great public attraction of all gatherings is the music. (Orson Parker, *The Fire and the Hammer: Revivals and How to Promote Them* [Boston: James H. Earle, Publisher, 1877], p. 47.)

Part II.

Campmeeting Spirituals: How They Happened

a. A New Kind of Hymn in a New Kind of Songbook

As one examines the campmeeting spirit, it is evident that the new religious experiences that were flaming hot in the first third of the nineteenth century in America must have demanded a new kind of hymn quite different from the solemn psalm tunes.

The spark that originally ignited this hymnic fire was the revival now known as the First Great Awakening, which struck America in the 1730s and 1740s. In the Northeast, the strong preacher was Jonathan Edwards; in 1739 the famed English revivalist George Whitefield swept the colonies with his fiery preaching. Among the results of this Awakening was a missionary effort among Indians; another was the early stirring of antislavery feeling; still another was the founding of schools and colleges.

For a time after the First Great Awakening, there was a lull in religious activity, and backsliding caused by an increase of materialism aroused during the Revolutionary War. In the 1790s, however, a new spurt of religious awareness took hold; and, especially in North Carolina, renewed revivals took place that reinforced the revolt against established forms of living and thinking. The strong sense of individual importance—the total man, a creature of feeling, and of value in the sight of God—had been the underlying philosophy of the Revolutionary War, and was leading families to turn to the new frontiers.

By the time of this Second Great Awakening, the Old Testament emphasis of the metric Psalms was failing to match the people's new attraction to the New Testament. "To Jesus!" was their cry. They sought the comfort of his promises of eternal life and salvation for the individual seeker.

A new kind of hymn was needed for this new feeling. Watts and Wesley and other eighteenth-century English hymnists had written hymns that expressed the emotions of the newly converted, and these were wholeheartedly adopted.[1] But new hymns, and especially new tunes, had to be found that equally conveyed the sense of the exhilaration, even the ecstasy, which newborn souls needed to express.

In answer, unnamed native hymnists wrote folkish poems, which began to come into print at the very end of the eighteenth century.

What is of especial moment here is when the early American folk hymn met the campmeeting exuberance, and some of the folk hymns evolved into campmeeting spirituals. Since with few exceptions the early writers about camp meetings are silent about the creative process that produced the campmeeting spirituals, one must turn to other sources for information. Among these is the campmeeting songbook, with its new-old words and tunes, and with its preface, where the compiler may give some hints about the use or origin of the songs.

Designed especially for camp meetings, little word-only books began to appear soon after the first camp meetings. They were often called "songsters," a most misleading term since no tunes were given.

The songsters[2] flourished earlier than the books with tunes and hence can give valuable clues about the emergence of the campmeeting song—even though the absence of the tunes can almost not be borne! Here one finds the crude, homemade lines written by anonymous campmeeting versifiers. The few names we are given are those of campmeeting preachers, and we may assume that many of the hymns were the product of the uneducated clergy of the frontier. Since most of the songsters were Methodist one can understand the lack of polish and the poor grammar of the uneducated itinerant.[3] But the spirit of the camp meeting is present, and even some of the physical details of the meetings are occasionally revealed in the verses.[4]

From the very first, the songsters included the words of the *choruses,* which are the distinctive feature of the campmeeting spiritual. (See Section II d-1 below.) The songsters also presented a great variety of meter, reflecting Charles Wesley's freedom from the old long, short, and common meters.

And the new tunes were also at hand, coming into print from two to four decades later than the first appearance of the words. They were in large part the folk ballads, love songs, and even the dance tunes (see Songs 2, 13, 17, 25, 29, 30, 37) that the Scotch-Irish immigrants had brought with them from the old country. Dance tunes? Yes! For as we shall see, these hymn singers used any tunes they knew, sacred or secular, to express their newfound joy.

Nobody knows, for records do not show, exactly when or how these secular tunes were first adapted to sacred words. Was it in Vermont?[5] George Pullen Jackson, dean of researchers in the field of American folk hymns, reached the conclusion in his *Down-East Spirituals* that many of the tunes were originally British, probably brought to western New England by the Baptists.[6] It was in one of their late eighteenth-century American hymnbooks that the folkish hymn texts were first printed which they sang to secular British airs and dance tunes. (To find out about the songbooks containing campmeeting spirituals, see Part III.)

The campmeeting spirituals spread like the kudzu vine, and soon covered the country with their catchy, fervent melodies. Although there were variations from place to place and from singer to singer, many of the campmeeting songs were widely known. We must assume, of course, that a great many were never recorded and have been lost to us.

St. James Fry wrote in 1859: "The most of these hymns are now entirely lost; for some of them were never written at all. Many of them existed a short time in the manuscript and in the memories of a few."[7] And half a century later, Lorenz expanded the thought:

> Unfortunately very few of these "spirituals" were ever published, and fewer still have survived the utter transformation of conditions during the last fifty years. . . . These "spirituals" are genuine folk songs. . . . The great danger is that nearly all record of a very interesting . . . product of the American musical church life will be lost.[8]

But there is a rich heritage. Here, in brief, is the probable story of the early folk hymn tunes: the adopting of familiar secular ballads and love songs from the old country, made over into melodies that fit homespun hymns or the beloved works of Watts and Wesley; their having been carried south from New England into Pennsylvania, Virginia, and the Carolinas; their being brought to camp meetings in the memories of the frontiersmen. When the camp meetings caught fire, these songs were the kindling.

What happened next? We can only guess. The singing aroused a mass response far more quickly than the most eloquent sermon, the most spirited exhortation. Was it perhaps the preacher who created the choruses? Or was it the congregation that went beyond the old hymn? At the end of the first line, set out by the preacher, was there a shout by an inflamed individual? Echoed by the crowd? A spontaneous melody enhancing the shout? The new response, or refrain, repeated at the end of the next line?

All we know is that somehow, in the heat of the revival fervor, the new songs were created, repeated, and passed on to other gatherings. The catchiest ones were remembered and the words written down and printed in the pocket-size songsters—and a new kind of hymnody was born. "It is the very nature of revival enthusiasm," wrote Louis Benson, "to develop its own song."[9]

The "wild and joyful songs"[10] were not static; they were rubbed smooth by much singing, the words and tune always being changed a little by each successive singer. We know too that by the early forties, when the tunes first began appearing in print in quantity, the compilers and editors of the new songbooks were polishing away much of what they considered to be the crudity of the original, and in the process sometimes removed other distinctive folk features. (See Part II d-5.)

Two early comments on the creation of campmeeting spirituals follow:

> Some preacher or local leader had an inspiration in the furnace heat of a meeting and produced a new chorus that was connected with an old hymn. If it struck fire, it was carried to the next camp meeting, or caught up by the itinerant or presiding elder, who sang it wherever he went, and so it was widely introduced.[11]

> Hymns, or "spiritual songs" as they more frequently were called, to the cultivated ear rude and bold in expression, rugged in meter and imperfect in rhyme, often improvised in the preaching stand, were at once accepted as more suited to their wants. These were quickly committed to memory, and to a considerable extent usurped the place of the older and more worthy hymns.[12]

In the South it was the singing-school masters who wrote down the campmeeting tunes because "they wanted to take advantage of their singability and popularity."[13] In the North many of the songsters and songbooks were compiled by preachers, with the same purpose.

The term "spiritual songs" had long been used to describe the personal act of worship, as opposed to the corporate. Now it was used to denote the folk hymns, and especially the campmeeting songs. Later, the adjective became a noun, and the folk hymns became "spirituals."[14] Lorenz was using the designation "American Spiritual" in his compilations by the 1880s. In the nineteenth century the term "For Social Worship" was employed in subtitles of songbooks to indicate meetings where the campmeeting spirituals would be sung.

b. Spirituals in Action

Once created, the campmeeting spirituals were sung and sung and sung. As we have seen, song filled the camp from morning till night till morning again. The songs "helped light revival fires";[15] they helped teach theology;[16] they were sung at home in family devotions;[17] they were sung at class meetings in answer to personal testimony.[18]

Before long a body of song had grown up that had been made a part of the informal services of almost all nonliturgical denominations. The Methodists and Baptists and Adventists may have been the most ardent singers of campmeeting spirituals, but they were not the only ones. There were, for example, the English Primitive Methodists, who, under the leadership of the American itinerant "crazy" Lorenzo Dow, adopted the style, and sang so heartily that a saying grew up, "You sing like a Primitive."[19]

Among the most enthusiastic proponents of campmeeting songs were the German denominations of Pennsylvania: the United Brethren, Evangelicals, and others.[20] They used the familiar campmeeting spirituals in German translations and partial borrowings and were among the first to publish campmeeting songsters. (See Section h, below.)

The Spiritualists and the Latter Day Saints adapted the spirituals to their own needs. Shakers had their own ecstatic songs, which paralleled those of the camp meetings; a Shaker convert, former Presbyterian Richard McNemar, wrote their first recorded songs.[21] As he had attended the Cane Ridge camp meeting, and heard the singing there, his words have a familiar ring. Shaker songs with choruses were rare, but other forms of revival usage, such as the textual *aaab* form (triple repetition followed by a short line), are to be found.[22] (See Song 43.)

The Holiness wing of Methodism virtually took over the Methodist camp meetings after the Civil War, and the later Methodist songbooks (*The Revivalist,* for example) reflect the Holiness tenets in some of the songs.

The relationship of campmeeting spirituals to Negro spirituals will be considered in Section g, below.

c. What People Said About Campmeeting Spirituals

Over a Century Ago

Congregational singing will never become general and permanent until the churches employ tunes which have melodies that cling to the memory and touch the feelings of the imagination. . . . In selecting music, we should not allow any fastidiousness of taste to set aside the lessons of experience. A tune which has always interested a congregation, which inspires the young, and lends to anthems a fit expression, ought not to be set aside because it does not follow the reigning fashion, or conform to the whims of technical science. There is such a thing as Pharisaism in music. Tunes may be very faulty in structure, and yet convey a full-hearted current that will sweep out of the way the worthless, heartless trash which has no merit except a literal correctness. And when, upon trial, a tune is found to do good work, it should be used for what it does, and can do. . . .

Not the least excellent are the popular revival melodies, which, although often excluded from classic collections of music, have never been driven out from among the people. They have been gathered up, fitly arranged, and having already performed most excellent service, they are now set forth with the best of all testimonials—the affection and admiration of thousands who have experienced their inspiration. Because they are homebred and popular, rather than foreign and stately, we like them none the less. And we cannot doubt that many of them will carry up to heaven the devout fervor of God's people until the millennial day! (Henry Ward Beecher, Preface to *Plymouth Collection,* 1856.)

This collection of music contains the best standard tunes . . . for ordinary congregational purposes, and an abundance of the lighter kinds, with stirring choruses, which quicken the emotions, and tend to mobilize religious singing. (Preface to *The Centenary Singer,* 1859.)

One characteristic of Methodist singing it should not lose, namely its extemporaneousness, spontaneity, the application in social worship of a single stanza or stirring chorus to a special case. (Erastus Wentworth, "Methodists and Music," *The Methodist Quarterly Review,* July, 1865, p. 374.)

A Half-Century Ago

"Purely emotional aim, . . . the crudity of its methods," making it "very harrowing to refined feelings and seemingly destructive of reverence." (Louis Benson, *The English Hymn,* 1915 p. 293.)

As a means of quickening the spirit of devotion, of confirming the faith of the believer, of enlivening his hope and increasing his zeal for the church, nothing, perhaps, exceeded the songs which resounded with the march of Methodism. (W. M. Gewehr, "Some Factors in the Expansion of Frontier Methodism, 1800–1811," *Journal of Religion,* January, 1928, p. 116.)

And Recently

Their simple words and images offered a key to the longings of the crowds which sang them, and their simple tunes and meters required no skill and therefore invited everyone to participate in the service. Yet precisely for this reason, they furnished a backbone to a revival meeting, and sometimes they were almost the meat of an entire revival in themselves. (Bernard A. Weisberger, *They Gathered at the River* [Boston: Little, Brown, 1958], p. 148.)

The camp meetings . . . were to demand a new type of song, untutored, lively, revivalistic. . . .

[The new converts'] joy in the gospel would have been quenched had they been denied the very hymns which mediated their ecstasy. . . . When the church in its official hymnals refused to recognize campmeeting songs . . . the paper-backed collection of "ephemeral" songs . . . would take over. (Fred Gealy, *Companion to the Hymnal: A Handbook to the 1964 Methodist Hymnal* [Nashville: Abingdon, 1970], pp. 37, 38.)

d. A Portrait of the Campmeeting Spiritual

This section and the rest of Part II will attempt to show the features of the campmeeting spiritual which give it its unique character. By the time you have read about the words and music, and have examined the songs of Part V, which illustrate the written description, you will be able to call them your friends.

1. The Refrain and the Chorus

What is the best way to make people start singing? Strike up the chorus! Although the refrain and the chorus (see Explanation of Terms) are not omnipresent in the campmeeting spiritual, they are its chief characteristic, and the main device whereby the great crowds at the camp meetings were helped to sing. People *needed* help, with no songbooks or instruments, not to mention silver screen or amplification systems!

Refrains of various kinds had been used in hymns before, but usually they were extensions growing out of the hymn itself, the words often changing with each successive stanza to fit its textual content. An example of this "extension refrain" is *Awake, my soul, in joyful lays* (Song 30), a hymn by Samuel Medley, which in campmeeting days was used with the tune "Loving-Kindness," a "Western Air" (meaning a tune from the Kentucky revivals). Notice how the final refrain varies with each stanza:

Example: (Stanza, line 2) He justly claims a song from me: His loving kindness O how free!
(Extension refrain) His loving kindness, loving kindness, His loving kindness O how free!

Extension refrains are found occasionally in campmeeting spirituals. (See also Songs 2, 29.)

But the "interrupting refrain" (a term coined for the present study) is quite different. Here is a campmeeting song that illustrates it. The italic words are the interrupting refrain:

Of him who did salvation bring, *He was found worthy,*
I could forever think and sing, *He was found worthy.*
Cho. O the bleeding Lamb, O the bleeding Lamb,
O the bleeding Lamb, *He was found worthy.*

The interrupting refrain is inserted at the end of each line of a stanza, and is sometimes found also at the end of the chorus. This refrain is often (but not always) completely unrelated to what comes before or after. (See also Songs 1, 14, 17, 18, 22, 23, 26, 31-34.)

The interrupting refrain demands special consideration, for it is an evidence of the "leader-and-response" form of folk music found in more cultures than just our own. It is, for instance, frequently present in African music, and thus became an important part of the Negro spiritual, such as: (Leader) Swing low, sweet chariot, (Response) *Comin' for to carry me home.* The leader-and-response form was not only the basis of the campmeeting spiritual, it is still being created today, as one can see by observing some of the so-called contemporary folk hymns. Austin Caswell suggests how it comes about:

The song leader and the congregation form the two structural elements of the performing group: the leader guides the progress of the song and introduces the verses in the order he chooses, while the congregation responds to him by picking up his cues and singing the rest of the verse he begins (if they know it), and providing the refrains at the end of the lines. . . .

Historical accounts tell us that this was not only the way that spiritual songs were learned but also the way they were created—new verses and new tunes being assembled on the spot with congregational refrains liberally applied as the glue to hold the entire structure together.[23]

George Pullen Jackson, whose five books on American sacred folk song cover just about every phase, confesses that no one knows much about the origin of the revival spirituals or their choruses. He writes in *White and Negro Spirituals:*

We do, however, know something of how crowds, all crowds, tend to handle a song. We know that they "come in" on the chorus; we know indeed that crowds sing nothing but the chorus, or an even briefer snatch like the short-phrase refrain, or any single line or couplet of the text which strikes their fancy. We are perfectly safe in projecting this present-day folk-selective condition backward 100 to 150 years. Hence we know that we must seek the essence of the campmeeting song contribution in those shorter or longer recurrent or repetitive passages.[24]

As one looks closely at these short, often ejaculatory refrains, it seems probable indeed that the interrupting refrains were generated by the campmeeting crowds in the tremendous excitement of the meetings, in response to the preacher's singing of the verses.

The campmeeting *chorus* is longer and more substantial than the refrain. (Sometimes it has no verses; these "independent choruses" will be considered under Section 3, below.) For spirituals with especially strong choruses, see Songs 2, 14, 17, 23, and 25. There are many, many others.

Among the choruses found most often are the following (the figures in parentheses indicate their number in the Song Examples of Part V): *And to glory I will go; Glory,*

glory, hallelujah (41); *Hallelujah to the Lamb; I do believe; I love Jesus; I will arise* (27); *I'm bound for the Kingdom; I am bound for the promised land* (25); *Jesus is my friend* (16); *O Canaan, bright Canaan* (31); *O how I love Jesus* (39); *O that will be joyful* (2); *O the Lamb* (24); *Palms of victory; Remember me; There'll be no sorrow (parting) there; Turn to the Lord* (6); *We are passing away; We'll stem the storm; We're going home;* and *Will you go* (32).

The choruses were catchy; they were popular because they were short, they were repetitive, they were rousing, and the words could easily be changed for denominational variance. They were spontaneously coupled to a hymn. Any one chorus could be coupled to a wide variety of hymns, and conversely, almost any one hymn could be used with a wide variety of choruses. For example, the popular chorus *O Canaan, bright Canaan* (Song 31) was found with nineteen different hymns in the songbooks studied.

Sometimes the choruses were sung before the stanzas, sometimes after. With only eight exceptions, all the songs of this study had the chorus following. The choruses of Pennsylvania Dutch campmeeting spirituals invariably come first; Lorenz gives the chorus first in all but one of his examples. The choruses were always sung first by the Advent Christians in New Hampshire. Jackson, on the other hand, lists the chorus first in only three of his two-hundred-plus examples.

A favorite textual form for the campmeeting choruses— indeed of folk songs of all kinds—is what we shall call the *aaab* pattern. A campmeeting example is Song 41:

> Say, brothers, will you meet us, (*a*)
> Say, brothers, will you meet us, (*a*)
> Say, brothers, will you meet us (*a*)
> On Canaan's happy shore. (*b*)

Easy to remember? Campmeeting songs had to be! (See the choruses of Songs 26, 37-41.) You know of this pattern in songs such as *Here we go round the mulberry bush, Skip to* my Lou, *We won't go home until morning, Glory, glory Hallelujah,* and even *Jesus Loves Me.*

A similar text-form is the *aaba* pattern, found often in Negro spirituals. A campmeeting example is Song 25:

I am bound for the promised land (*a*)
I am bound for the promised land (*a*)
O who will come and go with me (*b*)
I am bound for the promised land. (*a*)

(See Song 42, which combines these two patterns: *aaab* for the verse, *aaba* for the chorus. See also song 1.)

An early songster, *The Campmeeting Lyre,* also has several examples of the *aaba* text-form, including the following:

I'll never come back any more (2x)
I'll ride in the golden chariot in the morning,
I'll never come back any more.

O play on the golden harp (2x)
I want to go where Mary's gone
To play on the golden harp.

2. The "Mother-Hymn"

The term "mother-hymn" was coined for this study to denote the standard hymn (or portions of it) to which the chorus was affixed. (Jackson's term, "wandering couplet," does not always pertain.) It was mentioned above that a mother-hymn could be used with a variety of choruses, that a chorus could travel from one mother-hymn to another, and that the words were usually set to a folk hymn tune. A good illustration of a favorite mother-hymn is

Jesus, my all, to heaven is gone,
He whom I fixed my hopes upon.

This could be followed by a refrain: *We have a home in glory,* or *I want to live a Christian here,* or *O glory, glory to the Lamb,* or *Away over Jordan.* Again, a device for easy remembering!

Why did certain hymns win favor as mother-hymns, while other eighteenth-century hymns did not? Why was Charles Wesley's conversion hymn, *O for a thousand tongues to sing,* not chosen as a mother-hymn?

Here are the great favorites: (The numbers following the authors' names refer to Song Examples in Part V. See also Songs 1, 14, 18, 20, 31, 34, 35.)

Alas, and did my Savior bleed (Watts) (24)
Am I a Soldier of the Cross (Watts) (29)
Come, humble sinner, in whose breast (Jones)
Come, thou fount of every blessing (Robinson)
  (7 and others)
Come, ye sinners poor and needy (Hart) (27)
Jesus, my all, to heaven is gone (Cennick) (26, 33)
O land of rest, for thee I sigh (Mills?)
O when shall I see Jesus (Anon.)
On Jordan's stormy bank I stand (Stennett) (17)
There is a fountain filled with blood (Cowper)
There is a land of pure delight (Watts) (3)
When I can read my sentence clear (Watts)

To make mother-hymns easier to sing, they were often shortened and condensed into mere couplets, interrupted by refrains, combined with couplets from other hymns, and made all but unrecognizable. Yet sometimes they were also used intact. Here are two examples of the way a portion of a standard hymn was made into a mother-hymn, a vehicle for a refrain and a chorus. The interrupting refrains are in italic:

I have some friends before me gone,
For a few days, for a few days,
And I'm resolved to follow on,
For a few days, for a few days,

If you get there before I do,
For a few days, for a few days,

GLORY, HALLELUJAH!

Look out for me, I'm coming too,
For a few days, for a few days,
My suffering time will soon be o'er,
For a few days, for a few days,
Thus I shall sigh and weep no more,
For a few days, for a few days,

Farewell, vain world, I'm going home,
For a few days, for a few days,
My Savior smiles and bids me come,
For a few days, for a few days,

(*Chorus:* For I have a home up yonder.)

(*The Revivalist,* No. 20)

Beyond the bounds of time and space,
We have a home in glory.
Look forward to that heavenly place,
We have a home in glory.

Come on, my partners in distress,
We have a home in glory.
My comrades through the wilderness,
We have a home in glory.

Jesus my all to heaven is gone,
We have a home in glory.
He whom I fixed my hopes upon,
We have a home in glory.

(*Chorus:* O glory, glory! There's room enough in Paradise.)

(*The Revivalist,* No. 256)

As an illustration of the versatility of the mother-hymn, take *Alas, and did my Savior bleed.* It occurred seventy times in this present study of over two hundred songbooks and songsters, with seventeen different choruses, including five in *Devotional Melodies* alone. The chorus most often used (twenty times) is *O the Lamb, the loving (bleeding) Lamb.* The tune most often used is "Suffering Savior."

(See Song 24.) Nine of the occurrences of *Alas, and did my Savior bleed* have no chorus, but in these cases the tune given is a folk tune such as "Freeland" or a "Western Air."

It must not be assumed that the *tunes* sung to the mother-hymns were the same tunes considered "standard" in the eighteenth and nineteenth centuries or today. The tunes adopted have a folksy flavor; they sound like, and very likely sprang from, Irish or Scottish dance tunes or folk airs. And even these tunes were not constantly identified with the same mother-hymns.

3. The Independent Chorus

Independent choruses are the most fun of all the spirituals to sing! They are more like play-party songs than hymns. Sometimes this form of campmeeting spiritual may be quite long; sometimes it is only four measures. Here one finds no mother-hymn; words and music alike are campmeeting-generated. This is perhaps the kind of campmeeting spiritual that has persisted the longest and that tells us most about the camp meetings themselves.

The main characteristic of this kind of song is the great number of stanzas, ranging from six to thirty. No feat of memory is necessary to master these stanzas, for not only are they short, but usually all the words except one of each stanza are like all the other stanzas. The changing word was sometimes called the "family word."[25] The first stanza might tell something about the father, the next the mother, then sister and brother and preacher and sinner and mourner, and sometimes John Wesley or Noah or Daniel or any other person or group of people the crowd could think of spontaneously. There are dozens and dozens of spirituals with the family word; here is a good example:

1. My brother, I wish you well,
2. My sister, I wish you well,
3. My mother, I wish you well,

and so on for as many verses as the imagination can supply words for: Preachers? Members? Sinners?

Probably the most persistent use of the family word is *Where are the Hebrew Children* (Song 44), which takes us through almost the whole Bible! Indeed, the title of "Hebrew Worthies" is occasionally given to this song. (See also Songs 5, 9, 37, 40, 41, 46.)

Independent choruses frequently have one- or two-line stanzas, inviting new verses to be invented on the spot—rollicking good fun for the singers! (See Songs 8-10, 23, 40-43, 45-47.)

The most ubiquitous of the one-line choruses is *Come to Jesus* (Song 47a), consisting of the *aaab* pattern and innumerable verses seldom the same in any two hymnals. The tune is familiar to us through parodies. Another persistent independent chorus is *Say, brothers, will you meet us* (see Song 41 and its annotation); it too is irresistible as a basis for parodies.

The most spritely and creative of all campmeeting spirituals belong to this category of independent choruses. Some are found only in the songsters, and we may never know the tunes associated with them.

4. The Words of the Campmeeting Spirituals

A study of campmeeting texts as a whole (mother-hymns and choruses) indicates that they are limited to a few categories, on which the changes are rung. Subjects most frequently found are heaven and the pilgrimage there, love and praise to Jesus (almost never to God), world rejection, forgiveness and grace, repentance, atonement, and Last Judgment. This last subject was almost universal, for the Adventist movement was strong at the time the camp-meeting spirituals were developing, and the Second Coming was expected by nearly all Christians. The words of the choruses are a mishmash of Scripture, ejaculations, and borrowings from familiar hymns. They often have little or nothing to do with the text of the mother-hymn. In contrast to the chorus of the gospel song, the campmeeting chorus seldom rhymes; and, when rhymes do occur they are usually the slant rhyme of the primitive style, such as *too/below, bond/around.*

These texts are often shallow in their thought, never clever; they are seldom poetic, seldom oversentimental, always naïve and vigorous.

Ejaculations ("shouting words") are an important part of the refrains and choruses of campmeeting spirituals. Those most commonly found in northern spirituals are *Hallelujah! Glory! Save! Yes! Remember me,* and *Will you go.* They enhance the rhapsodic flavor of the songs. *Glory, glory, hallelujah!* is a persistent example.

Errors in grammar are found now and then, and are understandable when one thinks of the limited education of not only the frontier people but many of the itinerant preachers. "He learns the swearing man to pray," "He has died for you and I," and "My sin hath like a mountain rose" are examples found a number of times in various books.

Dialogue hymns were especially popular in both the eighteenth and nineteenth centuries. *Good Morning, Brother Pilgrim* is a dialogue between a scoffer and a believer. There are four dialogue hymns in *The Revivalist.* (See Songs 5, 12, 41.)

The *ballad* form, especially that relating a personal experience, was always enjoyed. From the secular ballad tradition, the stock opening phrase "Come all ye . . . " was taken over by the campmeeting spirituals. (See Song 13.)

The popularity of *parting songs* has already been mentioned. (See Section b of Part I, and Songs 2-5.)

A kind of *limerick form* (of all things!) is found in *Revival Hymns,* 1843. These seem to get into trouble in the final line—no rhyming dictionaries on the frontier!

The work of the Lord doth revive / In grace and in knowledge we thrive / Our hearts God is touching / The day is approaching / Sing glory, hallelujah, Amen.

Our Lord is a prayer-hearing Lord / For Jesus hath spoken the word / That all true believers / By prayer are receivers / Of pardon. O seek it just now.

5. The Music of the Campmeeting Spirituals

The *vocal range* is wide, often extending an octave and a half. (See Song 5, 13, 31.) Low B's, and high G's and even A's are found. This was not uncommon for the times, especially in the ballads to be sung by a soloist, but for mass singing it seems odd to us who are accustomed to hymn tunes contained within an octave.

A favorite musical form was to let the chorus repeat the music of the verse. Another way of simplifying the learning process! (See Songs 1, 24, 25, 34, 35.)

Because the compilers of the Northern campmeeting songbooks usually were untrained musicians, they often made mistakes in writing rhythm. Errors are most often found in tunes of 3/2 time, a favorite meter.

The music of the campmeeting spirituals seldom contains any accidental sharps or flats. Most of the Northern ones are in major keys; those from the Pennsylvania Dutch country are almost always in major.

There are, however, quite a few examples of campmeeting spirituals based on scales besides our familiar major and minor modes. These frequently include natural minor, or the Aeolian mode, and less often the Dorian mode or the Mixolydian mode. Study the examples below, and also the songs of Part V that are in the Aeolian (Songs 1, 10, 14, 16, 17, 27, 48b); Dorian (Songs 18-20); and Mixolydian (Song 22) modes. These three modes are found widely in all sorts of folk songs.

Unfortunately, Northern editors often thought the use of these modes was a mistake made by folk-hymn singers who sang the tunes to the editors, who would then "correct" them, so to speak, by adding chromatics that made the tune plain minor. Southern editors were seldom guilty of this tampering with the folk quality of the modal spirituals.

Often the scales would be incomplete, or "gapped," with fewer than seven tones—a missing *fa* or *ti* or both. Pentatonic, or five-toned, melodies are found in both major and minor modes, as for instance the familiar tune to "Amazing Grace," based on *do re mi sol la*—no *fa* or *ti*. Pentatonic tunes, common to many cultures around the world, are an almost universal musical language. (See Songs 13, 28, 29, 48a.)

In the beginning, campmeeting spirituals were transmitted orally, and not put into print until decades after they were created. One therefore finds in them traces of the style of the folk-song singer. Earnest editors sometimes tried to record the slurs, pauses, and irregularities of those who sang the songs their grandfathers and -mothers had sung to them. But no ordinary notation can convey the embellishments, the quarter tones, the slides, and the free rhythm of the singers themselves. Several of the campmeeting songbooks will mark in the top right-hand corner of the music, "As sung by"—and the music will be full of folkish slide effects and holds or extended note-values. Notable among such books of the North are *The Revivalist* and *Sacred Melodies for Social Worship*. (For songs exhibiting the characteristics of the folk-song singer, see 11, 16, 19, 48a, 48b.)

Lorenz complains that trying to write down folk hymns as they are sung can be frustrating:

As [the campmeeting song] was . . . orally transmitted, little changes were often made in the melody until it met the needs of the popular consciousness. . . . There were a good many grace notes and slurred passing notes in their solos that it would be difficult to reproduce on a staff. . . . I remember [hearing] an old local preacher sing . . . with great earnestness over forty years ago in the foothills of the Alleghanies. . . . I remember that it was minor and intensely sad, full of slurrings and quaverings.[26]

Finally, in this capsule description of the campmeeting spiritual, there is one song that presents many of the aspects discussed: "I Can't Stay Away." (See Song 1 in Part V.)

Note that the chorus comes before the verse, and the music of the chorus is the same as that of the verse. A rhyming couplet constitutes the mother-hymn (*Jesus, my all*). The words describe the journey to heaven; the refrain text is a modified *aaba* pattern. There is an interrupting refrain (*I can't stay away*). The melody is in the Aeolian mode (natural minor); there is no *fa* in the scale, and there are no accidentals.

6. The Campmeeting Hymn

There are many hymns, in general less effervescent than those just examined, which may be claimed for the camp meeting either because (a) they were written specifically for camp meetings, or (b) because they were already familiar to the campmeeting attendants and so beloved of them that the songs appear in the majority of the revival songbooks. Both of these kinds of hymns were sung, presumably, to tunes already familiar to the crowd. Among the hymns were dialogues, personal experiences, and ballads.

The favorite topics of the ones written especially for camp meetings included (1) unceasing, vigilant warfare (the camp grounds were set up like a military camp); (2) items of orthodox doctrine: Christ's sacrifice, his second coming, heaven, hell, and death; and (3) Holiness (an emphasis increasing toward the middle of the century).[27]

Many of these hymns, especially those found in the early songsters, were written by unknown frontier poets under the inspiration of the occasion. The terminology often points directly to the camp meeting. They are usually crude, sometimes ungrammatical, and with faulty rhymes. Few of them endured.

We *do* know the names of a few of the pioneer hymnists: Peter Cartwright (see Section c of Part I), Enoch Mudge, B. W. Gorham, Caleb Taylor, and, most famous of all, John Granade, a moody preacher of Methodism's Kentucky and Tennessee circuits. His hymns were widely used and freely altered, even mutilated. Books as early as Hinde's *Pilgrim's Songster* (Ohio, 1815) and as late as

Hauser's *Olive Leaf* (Georgia, 1878) made much of his work, as does the 1859 article by Fry, already cited here.

Two of Granade's most popular hymns were: *Hark! listen to the trumpeters / They call for volunteers* (based on a military theme, so popular with post-Revolutionary Kentuckians), and *Sweet rivers of redeeming love / Lie just before mine eyes.* The first of these was used as a mother-hymn with the refrain *I mean to go;* the second was kept intact as a hymn.

There are many favorite hymns found in campmeeting songbooks that were not campmeeting-generated. These are usually hymns by the eighteenth-century English hymnists, and the tunes to which they were sung in camp meetings were folk tunes, probably of British origin. Typical of this kind of hymn is *Amazing Grace* (Song 48), for which there are several pleasing folkish tunes. Other tunes beloved of the camp meetings were "Pleading Savior" (21), "Holy Manna" (28), "Pisgah" (29), "Loving-Kindness" (30), "Garden Hymn," and "Expostulation." (Figures in parentheses refer to Song Examples in Part V.)

Three *composed* tunes are notable for their persistence and popularity in campmeeting songbooks and today's hymnals. One is "Beloved" (*O thou in whose presence*), by John Swain and Freeman Lewis. Another is "Maitland," also known as "Cross and Crown," written in 1846 by George Allen, and almost universally set to *Must Jesus bear the cross alone.* These tunes are frequently attributed in the nineteenth-century songbooks as "Western Air," thus revealing their campmeeting usage. Almost equally popular was the composed song *O happy day,* by the Englishman E. F. Rimbault. These three are hereby nominated as "honorary campmeeting spirituals."

e. Secular Tunes Put to a New Use

Besides the British folk tunes, the campmeeting and revival people put to use the popular secular songs of their day. Does it shock you, the idea of singing sacred words to (for instance) "Home, Sweet Home" or a Stephen Foster favorite? It should not, for borrowing secular tunes as hymns was nothing new: it is a long-proven technique for getting people to sing. Secular music has been commandeered for use with sacred words from the very beginnings of Protestantism[28] (Luther adapted secular folk songs as chorales), and long before that in Catholic motets, where even the secular words were retained.[29] In revivals of religion a conscious effort is made to employ *any* tune that will encourage the people to sing. That the early English Methodists accepted the songs of the "pot and public houses," singing them in the "original lively time," seems hard to reconcile with John Wesley's edict that only the songs of the official hymnbooks should be sung by his people.[30] Sometimes popular appeal supercedes authoritarianism! (See Section b-1 of Part III.)

Among the popular tunes most frequently borrowed for the revival songbooks in the middle of the nineteenth century were those of Stephen Foster. (He also wrote a sizable number of very sentimental Sunday-school songs.) The Foster songs found most frequently with sacred words are: *Old Black Joe; My Old Kentucky Home; Hard Times, Come Again No More;* and *Massa's in the Cold, Cold Ground.* Others found less often are *O Susanna* and *Old Folks at Home.* Some students of the period are convinced that Foster had been more influenced by white sacred folk song than by Negro.[31]

Here are a few of the popular songs sung in revivals and camp meetings, with sacred words:

> *Annie Laurie:* My God, my life, my love.
> *Auld Lang Syne:* Hark! from the tombs a doleful sound.
> *Home, Sweet Home:* Mid scenes of confusion and creature complaints.
> *Long, Long Ago:* Shed not a tear o'er your friend's early bier/When I am gone.

My Old Kentucky Home: There is a land of pure delight.

'Tis the last rose of summer: 'Tis the last call of mercy.

And with typical campmeeting abandon, *She'll be coming round the mountain:* I'm going back to Jesus when he comes.

The preface to a songster of 1858, *The Chorus* (Philadelphia), tells us: "Whenever [the early Methodists] found that the devil had got a good tune that seemed to charm the people, someone immediately composed a hymn or spiritual song to that tune, and thus cheated Satan out of both tune and singers."

f. Parodies of Campmeeting Spirituals

The widespread popularity of the campmeeting songs was attested to by their parodies. Take, for instance, *Say, brothers, will you meet us* (Song 41): its early history as a campmeeting song with the refrain *Glory, glory, hallelujah* bespeaks its appeal. Then the execution of John Brown a year after the raid at Harper's Ferry (1858) called forth the first parody, *John Brown's body lies a-mouldering in the grave.* Sigmund Spaeth cites the possibility that this version may have originated at Fort Warren, Boston, in 1859, where the glee club liked the song and sang it on their way south. "Soon all the Union soldiers were taking it up, and *Glory, Hallelujah* became the marching song of the Northern armies." There were objectionable parodies after that, but "it remained for Julia Ward Howe to solve the problem and create a poem that is today recognized as perhaps the most distinguished among all our national hymns" (*Battle Hymn of the Republic*).[32]

In *The Revivalist* there are other religious parodies of *Say, brothers: Ye soldiers of the cross arise,* and *Now I know what makes me happy.* Later secular parodies are *John Brown's Baby, Little Peter Rabbit, It isn't any trouble just to S-M-I-L-E,* and still others beloved of pep-song leaders.

Almost as popular for parodying is *Come to Jesus* (Song 47), as *Clementine* and *Found a Peanut*. Another is *How pleasant thus to dwell below* (Song 2), which became *The man who has plenty of good peanuts*, still carrying the *O that will be joyful* refrain. These are with us still. The parody on *One more river to cross* (Song 34) is well known. There is a campmeeting chorus beginning *O you must be a lover of the Lord*, which was parodied as follows:

> O you must be a lover of the landlady's daughter
> Or you can't have a second piece of pie.[33]

It seems a cycle is completed: popular secular songs are made into hymns, and popular hymns are again made into secular songs through parodies.

A different kind of take-off, this a humorous one on the camp meetings rather than on the spirituals, was written by Mark Twain in his *Huckleberry Finn* (Chapter 20).

g. Camp Meetings: Cradle of Negro Spirituals?

(A Symposium of Opinion)

As we have seen (Section b of Part I), from the very beginning the blacks were active in the campmeeting scene, sharing in all phases of the excitement. And the chief cause and result of the excitement was the singing. Still a subject of dispute is whether the Christianization of the Negroes changed their singing. James Weldon Johnson says, "It was the force of Christianity on their lives that changed Negro music from barbaric tom-tom and drums and shouting to the music of the spirituals."[34]

What did they sing? Did their spirituals come from the campmeeting songs, or did the campmeeting songs derive from the Negro spirituals? This is another continuing argument that may never be solved. The earliest book of Negro spirituals (1867) says, "It is likely that Negro spirituals embody many reminiscences of the revival melodies of the south."[35] Some writers believe they can document the flow of song from white to black.[36] Newman White is the strongest and most convincing defender of that theory.[37]

But Miles Mark Fisher argues against it, for he believes that the spirituals were not folk music, but composed in order to encourage the field workers to work harder.[38] He also makes a strong case that the entire message of the spiritual is told in secret symbols about freedom—announcing an escape in *Go tell it on the mountain,* or demanding freedom in *Go down, Moses,* or yearning for a return to Africa in *Swing low, sweet chariot.*

Is it not probable that Fisher underestimates the religious fervor of the blacks—a fervor that may have led to their creation of spirituals in the camp meetings? John Work asserts the deep religious spirit of the blacks.[39]

But Dena J. Epstein, perhaps today's best scholar in the field, has this temperate opinion about what happened at camp meetings:

There is no room for doubt that blacks and whites worshipped and sang together in an atmosphere highly charged with emotion at camp meetings during the first half of the nineteenth century. That the participants were mutually influenced seems inescapable. Songs, parts of songs, and ways of singing must have been exchanged, without the excited folk knowing or caring who started what. The assumption that the blacks learned all their songs from the whites has not been proved, nor has documentation been found to prove the opposite.[40]

My own study of camp meetings confirms the enthusiasm of the blacks for the camp meetings, where their almost ceaseless singing, and the ecstasy that singing produced, emphatically suggest that the Negroes were sharing wholeheartedly in the religious experiences of the camp meeting, and that their spirituals were sincerely and genuinely religious. But no proof was found as to which came first, the white or the black.

A comparison of the words and music of Negro spirituals with incipits of Northern campmeeting songs shows thirty-two campmeeting songs that have titles and/or melodies similar to those of Negro spirituals. The campmeeting songs most nearly parallel to black spirituals are *Give me Jesus* (42); *O brother, be faithful* (40); *Old-time religion; Remember me; Roll, Jordan Roll; Roll on, sweet moments;* and *Old Ship Zion* (12). Many others of the forty-eight Song Examples of Part V suggest a Negro spiritual parallel. (See Songs 9, 17, 23, 27, 28, 34, 39, 41, 44, 46, 47a.)

The present study leads to a few tentative generalizations in the comparison of white campmeeting songs and Negro spirituals. In the Negro songs:

(a) The chorus comes first much more often.

(b) There is more frequent use of modes, syncopation, and free melody.

(c) The words are more imaginative, more poetic, more dramatic, more humorous.

(d) There is the same kind of repetition, but more variety of shouting words.

(e) There is almost never a mother-hymn.

(f) There are fewer refrains in the *aaab* form, but with more freedom, as:

Everywhere I go / Everywhere I go / Everywhere I go, my Lord / Somebody's talking about Jesus; *or,* O what a mourning (3x) When the stars begin to fall; *or,* Lord, make me more patient (3x) Until we meet again.

(g) There are more refrains in the *aaba* textual form, as:

We will march through the valley in peace / We will march through the valley in peace / If Jesus himself be our leader / We will march through the valley in peace; *or,* I can't stay behind, my Lord / I can't stay behind / There's room enough in the heaven, my Lord / I can't stay behind; *or,* I'm-a trouble in the mind (2x) / I ask my Lord what shall I do / I'm-a trouble in the mind.

(h) There is about the same proportion of use of the family word, with more occurrences of *brother, sister, mourner,* but less variety otherwise.

(i) There is a reasonable likelihood that the Negro spirituals had more influence on the Southern campmeeting songs than on the Northern.

(j) There is far more parallelism in the texts of the two cultures than in the music.

h. Pennsylvania Dutch "Bushmeeting" Spirituals Compared to Campmeeting Spirituals

The central part of Pennsylvania has always been known as being active in evangelical religion. With its concentration of German immigrants, the German-speaking churches persisted for a long time; the Evangelical Association and the United Brethren in Christ were among the sects that made the most use of the "bushmeeting" (German campmeeting) choruses. Don Yoder, in an extensive study in *Pennsylvania Spirituals,* and Albert F. Buffington, in his earlier *Dutchified German Spirituals*[41] (considerably smaller in scope), have listed the most popular Pennsylvania Dutch bushmeeting songs, most of which were translated quite literally from the English-language campmeeting spirituals.

The Pennsylvania Dutch bushmeeting spirituals are almost all in the major; the chorus always comes first; there is the same borrowing from popular secular songs *(Camptown Races, Vive l'amour, O dear, what can the matter be);* and in contrast to campmeeting songs, tune sequences are frequent. There are a few texts in the *aaab* style so prevalent in English-language campmeeting songs, but more in the *aaba* form found more often in Negro spirituals:

Yoder No. 78 (Yoder's phonetic spelling) (*aaba* form):

Meini heimet ist nicht heer   (*a*)
Meini heimet ist nicht heer   (*a*)
Ich weiss eini besseri heimet oss dees,   (*b*)
Meini heimet ist nicht heer.   (*a*)
(My home is not here.)

Yoder No. 91 (*aaab* form):

> O Harr, shenk oons de gnawdi,   (*a*)
> O Harr, shenk oons de gnawdi,   (*a*)
> O Harr, shenk oons de gnawdi,   (*a*)
> O shenk oons de gnawdi foon himmel har. (*b*)
>   (O Lord, send us a blessing.)

About three dozen of the bushmeeting spirituals listed by Yoder closely resemble campmeeting spirituals found in English-language songbooks, including *Say, brothers, will you meet us* (Song 41), *My brother's going to wear that crown* (Song 46), and *Come to Jesus* (Song 47).

There are still camp meetings being held in central Pennsylvania where these songs are sometimes sung in Pennsylvania Dutch. The Mt. Lebanon campground near Lebanon is an example.

i. A Comparison of Northern and Southern Campmeeting Spirituals

In comparing the body of Northern spirituals with that of the South, several possibilities come to mind. The first concerns their shared appearances. Are there many songs found only in the North? In the South? What proportion of the total is found in the songbooks of both areas?

The answer here is that it is almost impossible to judge accurately. There are so many variants, so many different tune names, so many different song-texts, that one cannot make a thorough study. Still, a few facts come forth. There are nineteen campmeeting spirituals in *The Revivalist* that could not be matched to tunes in *The Southern Harmony;* there were seventeen campmeeting tunes in the Southern book *The Good Old Songs* that found no certain counterpart in *The Revivalist*. This leaves a large number that are shared by both areas (with expected variations of both text and tunes).

The second phase of comparison deals with musical and textual matters. Is the Southern group freer in rhythm? Are there more shouting words (*Glory, Hallelujah, Yes,* and the like)—possibly because of the closer influence of Negro music?

Are the Northern songs more four-square in their form—possibly because of the concentration of musically well-trained German immigrants there? Or possibly because of the domination over the North exercised by Lowell Mason, with his firm ideas of "correctness" and his crusade for simple, regular hymn tunes?

Yes, the music and text of the *average* Northern songbooks are more sedate in form and melody than the Southern books, though the number and richness of shouting words is approximately the same. However, both Northern and Southern songs are far behind the Negro spirituals in shouting words.

Not *all* Northern songbooks and songs, however, are more sedate. *The Revivalist* and *Sacred Melodies for Social Worship,* for instance, both are pointed in the direction of oral transmission (see Section d-5, above). There, free melody is achieved by passing tones, and free rhythm by holds and "gathering notes" (see Explanation of Terms), usually found more often in Southern books. See the excerpt from the Southern *Sacred Harp,* below, with its two gathering notes (a) and its phrase extension (b).

"We'll Stem the Storm" *Sacred Harp,* 378

But no Southern hymn tune could be more fluent, more poetic, than the Northern version of *Jesus is my friend* (Song 16), found in three Northern books but in none of the Southern books consulted. Compare the tame melody of the Southern book *Good Old Songs,* below, with the poignant tune of Song 16 in Part V.

"Jesus Is My Friend" *Good Old Songs,* 652 (Refrain only)

Je - sus is my friend, O hal - le - lu - jah! Je - sus is my friend.

69

The campmeeting spirituals in most of the other leading Northern songbooks of the 1850s and later, however, have been edited into regular four-measure phrases and strict time.

What about the employment of modal melodies? Are they more common in the books of the cloistered Southern uplands than in those of the bustling urban Northeast? (English folk song, long cherished in our South, is rich in modal tunes.)

Yes, there is much greater use of modal music in the South than in the North. This is partly due to the tendency of the Northern editors to make over the modes into minor by raising the seventh. (See Section d-5, above.) This process is quite evident, for instance, in *The Revivalist,* where twenty-seven tunes, which in Southern versions were Aeolian, Dorian, or Mixolydian, were give accidentals to make the "strange-sounding" notes "right" (plain minor) for the editorial ears. Even so, there are many modal tunes remaining in the Northern campmeeting songbooks. The suspicion that German forthrightness might have influenced the Northern singers was probably legitimate mostly in the case of the Pennsylvania Dutch spirituals; they were (with almost negligible exception) strongly in the major, and in four-measure phrases. (See Section h, above.)

Part III.

Campmeeting Spirituals Come into Print

a. These Campmeeting Songbooks Were Pioneers

1784. The first of the songsters to contain folkish *texts* was Joshua Smith's *Divine Hymns and Spiritual Songs,* New Hampshire. This little book, compiled by a Baptist layman, was quite popular and went into several editions. In the 1811 edition, used for this study, there are twenty-three hymns of folkish nature.

1805. Jeremiah Ingalls, a singing-school master of Vermont, published his *Christian Harmony,* the first tunebook (see Explanation of Terms, p. 131) containing a goodly number of folk-hymn tunes. David Klocko, who is a specialist in *The Christian Harmony,* believes that some of its campmeeting songs may have been composed by Ingalls in the folk style for use in local camp meetings.[1] Hymnologist William J. Reynolds recognizes *The Christian Harmony* as "the first publication of these 'Old Baptist' folk melodies";[2] and Jackson writes:

> In deciding on the basic character of his projected *Christian Harmony,* [Ingalls] must have had his ear to the ground, that ground which had long shaken with the tread of the Merry Dancing Baptists and their Shaker kindred. His idea was to furnish those lively folk with a tune book of their beloved songs. . . . He actually gathered and published no less than eighty of their favorite hymn texts and as many of the tunes to which they had presumably been sung.[3] [See Song 6.]

Fifteen of *Christian Harmony's* thirty songs of camp-meeting character are also found in the 1868 Methodist songbook *The Revivalist*—the same words, same tune, or both. Eleven hymns in *Christian Harmony* have choruses or ejaculations characteristic of campmeeting spirituals, including *O hallelujah. The Christian Harmony*, although a landmark book, was not directly influential in its own area, but the next publication was, indeed.

1813. In this year, John Wyeth, a printer in Harrisburg, Pennsylvania, issued his *Repository of Sacred Music Part Second.* This book reflects the spread of folk hymns west and south of New England along the Appalachian ridges, as the settlers pushed first to Pennsylvania and later to the Carolinas and beyond.[4] It influenced the Southern tunebooks of the next several decades.

Irving Lowens, who prepared the facsimile edition, says in his Preface, "Part Second was something new in the tunebook field, an attempt to supply the musical needs of the vast market created by the revivals and camp meetings so prevalent in Pennsylvania at the time."[5] Here are nine hymns frequently found in campmeeting songbooks, and of those, four have choruses in the best campmeeting tradition. (See Song 7.)

This book was the important source of folk hymns for the Supplement to *Kentucky Harmony* (1820) and the later Southern tunebooks. (See Section b-4, below.) Aside from the three early Northern tunebooks discussed above and just below, the Southern tunebooks were almost the only publications to contain folk-hymn tunes until the 1840s. Only then did other Northern collections of revival tunes begin appearing in considerable numbers.

1831. But in the meantime, *The Christian Lyre*, by Jonathan Leavitt, a Congregational minister and ardent abolitionist, came into print and eventually went into twenty-six editions. This was virtually the first publication of *revival* tunes in any quantity; there are twenty with choruses and ten others of campmeeting character. (See Songs 4 and 47b.) The Preface is revealing:

"Every person conversant with revivals must have observed, that whenever meetings for prayer and conference assume a special interest, there is a desire to use hymns and music of a different character from those ordinarily heard in the church." Other songbooks fail to supply such tunes, he says, and *The Christian Lyre* has undertaken to fill that want.

b. Campmeeting Songbooks of the Denominations, from 1840

1. The Methodists

It is hard to believe, but true, that officially, the Methodists never accepted the camp meetings and never sanctioned a single revival songbook. Why not? Strange, when one remembers the Wesleys' eagerness to put to their use any tunes whatsoever that would entice the people into singing. It is equally inexplicable in view of the Methodists' resounding success in holding camp meetings and singing campmeeting songs.

There were rules and warnings ("We most earnestly entreat you, if you have any respect for the authority of the conferences, or of us, . . . to purchase no hymn books, but that are signed with the names of your bishops.")[6] But despite them all, Methodist songsters began to appear in the early years of the nineteenth century, and Methodist revival songbooks poured from the presses in the fifties and sixties, and nobody but the bishops seemed to pay any attention to the rules. *The Revivalist,* 1868, outshone all the Methodist songbooks in its richness of campmeeting songs.

2. The Revivalist, and Other Methodist Campmeeting Songbooks

The two hundred campmeeting spirituals of *The Revivalist* illustrate all phases of this most purely American of all folk hymns, and may well be the most important resource for their study.[7] *The Revivalist* is significant in its signpost position of looking back on one era and forward to a new one. For with the advent of the gospel song, just coming into prominence in the years covered by the editions of *The Revivalist,* a long period of new activity by songwriters and publishers was to begin. It was a time in which the exuberance and naïveté of the revival spiritual was to give way to the increasing sentimentality and unparalleled commercial exploitation of the composed ephemeral hymns. This trend is already evident in *The Revivalist's* supply of gospel songs, but there had not yet been time for it to effect the abandonment of the folk hymns.

Other Outstanding Methodist Songbooks Containing Campmeeting Spirituals: *Wesleyan Psalmist,* 1842; *Lute of Zion,* 1853; *Devotional Melodies,* 1859; *Sacred Melodies for Social Worship,* 1859; *Hallowed Songs,* 1866; *Centenary Singer,* 1867; *The New Song,* 1875. Also the *Methodist Hymnal,* 1966.

3. The Baptists

There were important Baptist songbooks published in the North by leading revivalists Jacob Knapp (1845) and A. B. Earle (1865), and later music leaders.

The Primitive Baptists carried on the campmeeting-song tradition longer than almost any sect. Their *Hymn and Tune Books* of 1879 and 1902 are cornucopias of beautiful folk hymns and revival folk songs.

Outstanding Baptist Songbooks Containing Camp-meeting Spirituals: *Evangelical Harp,* 1842; *Revival Hymns,* 1845; *Songs of Devotion,* 1870; *Baptist Praise Book,* 1872; *Baptist Hymn and Tune Book,* 1873.

4. Southern Tunebooks

Although this study is principally concerned with Northern spirituals and songbooks (see Preface), the early Southern tunebooks and songbooks must be mentioned here, if only briefly.

A few years after the publication of Wyeth's *Repository Part Second,* Ananias Davisson issued his *Kentucky Harmony,* a Methodist tunebook derived in part from Wyeth. Its Supplement, 1820, was the first of a Southern series of folk-hymn treasuries, mostly Baptist, all of which reflect the camp meeting to a greater or lesser extent: *Southern Harmony* (1835), *Sacred Harp* (1844), *Social Harp* (1855), *Olive Leaf* (1878), and others, each with more than thirty campmeeting songs.

5. The Adventists

The Adventists also had their offering of campmeeting songbooks. The steady and widespread rise of millennial hopes in the first half of the nineteenth century makes a story of dramatic power. The expectation of a Second Coming was felt not only by William Miller's followers, but by most of the denominations. Half of the Adventists had originally been Methodists.[8] The hopes of all centered on converting the whole country before the millennium. Almost all hymnody of the second quarter of the nineteenth century was colored by millennialist thought.

The Adventists wholeheartedly adopted the revival style of singing and hymn-making, and published many revival songbooks from the 1840s on, with great success. These books contained many campmeeting spirituals, some adapted to the special tenets of the Adventists, who contributed new ones of their own to the revival hymnody. Many of these songs describe the Last Judgment in lurid terms. Several of their unique songs were widely reprinted in songbooks of other denominations. (See Songs 8-10, 15.)

Especially in the 1840s, the Adventists gave new impetus to the singing in the North.[9] In published output, they came nearer to matching the Methodists than any other denomination. Even the overwhelming disappointment of the failure of their predictions could not stop them; from those days to the present the Adventists have sung their versions of the old campmeeting spirituals, and added their contribution of similar songs. Their hymnal of 1887 contained over fifty of them.

Outstanding Adventist Songbooks Containing Campmeeting Spirituals: *Millennial Harp,* 1846; *Jubilee Harp,* 1866; *Seventh-Day Adventist Hymn and Tune Book,* 1887;

New Jubilee Harp, 1888, *Seventh-Day Adventist Church Hymnal,* 1941.

6. The United Brethren in Christ; Evangelicals

The United Brethren in Christ had a long tradition of song. At first a part of the Pennsylvania Dutch community, they started publishing hymnbooks in 1808, in German, but soon (sooner than their Evangelical cousins) in English. Unlike the Methodists, their leaders welcomed the inclusion of revival hymns in their books. In spite of the modest size of the denomination, their strong publishing program provides an opportunity for studying camp-meeting songs almost equal to that of the Methodists.

The Evangelical Church, which later merged with the United Brethren, included in their hymnal of 1897 one hundred choruses "for ejaculatory use."

Outstanding United Brethren Songbooks Containing Campmeeting Spirituals: *American Church Harp,* 1856; *Hymns for the Sanctuary,* 1874; *Songs of Grace,* 1879 (quoted in the Jackson studies); *Otterbein Hymnal,* 1891.

7. Other Denominations

There were other denominations that published song-sters and songbooks containing substantial numbers of campmeeting spirituals, or songs in the campmeeting tradition. The various sects making up the Pennsylvania Dutch community have already been mentioned, as have the *Mormons* and the *Shakers.*

The Salvation Army, both in England and the United States, was greatly influenced by the campmeeting choruses, and created new ones for their songbooks, although like the Shakers they did not adopt many of the ones used by the campmeeting crowds.

A remarkable *Congregational* (really nondenomina-tional) hymnal of 1856 was the *Plymouth Collection,* published under the supervision of Henry Ward Beecher and his brother Charles. It contained over two dozen revival hymns, as well as the most noble hymns of all times. See page 46 for a quotation from its Preface.

The book was very popular and has been called the first official hymn-and-tune book for congregational use.[10] It did not go without criticism: someone said it was better suited for Christy's Minstrels than for church![11]

Other songbooks containing campmeeting spirituals were the *Prayer Meeting Hymn Book,* 1859 (Church of God), and the *Salvation Army Tune Book* (no date) (English).

8. Sunday-School Songbooks

Besides the songbooks, songsters, and an occasional tunebook, one can find campmeeting hymns in still another source, seldom tapped. This is the Sunday-school songbook, a type of publication that swept the country when the small volumes came on the market in the late 1850s. Originally designed for children (although one would scarcely recognize the fact when finding the many hymns of death and hell and general gloom), these collections contained not only the earliest gospel songs but also campmeeting songs in varying numbers.

Gospel songbooks (1875 and thereafter) also contained campmeeting spirituals. (See Sections a and b of Part IV.)

Part IV.

The Persistence of the Spirit of the Camp Meetings and Their Songs

One of the most rewarding phases of a study of campmeeting songs is to trace their persistence, both in later hymnals and in various outcroppings of the camp-meeting spirit. The campgrounds have become Chautauquas, the revivalists have turned professional, the song-books and songsters are now collectors' items. There are strong churches and colleges in what was then the wilderness. But what remains is the recurrent and persistent *spirit* of the meetings and of their songs.

This spirit may be likened to a great tree, with deep, strong roots and many large and sturdy branches. The tree is growing in soil that is centuries old, perhaps as old as man himself—soil that goes back to the time of rhapsodic primitive religions with such music (or other forms of expression) as the Jewish cantors still sing, or the Hindu mantras, or the Gregorian chants of the early Christian church—singing that is pure ecstasy. Religious revivals of all history have given similar expression in one way or another; those of Wesley and Edwards and Whitefield were the immediate predecessors of the camp meetings, and displayed some of the same emotional outbursts.

The trunk of this particular tree is the spirit of the campmeeting songs, and its branches represent different phases of that spirit evidenced in other aspects of American religious and secular life.

The campmeeting spirit has branched out in ways that are predictable, like the gospel songs. Other branches are happy surprises, like the contemporary "folk hymns" and the recently instituted congregational participation in the

Roman Catholic churches. Basically, this spirit is an expression of belief in the individual, his sense of the importance of his emotions, and the joy that comes in giving musical expression to those emotions—expression to which he feels he cannot give voice in a formal, dignified way, but more naturally in the circumstances and vocabulary of everyday living.

We have climbed the tree, so to speak, in some of the foregoing pages; now let us trust our weight to some of the branches.

a. The First Branch: The Sunday School Songs

The American Sunday School Union was founded in 1824, and soon began ambitious campaigns to supply materials to the Sunday schools that were being started all over the country, from the Atlantic to the newest frontier. The distribution of its Sunday-school literature led to the establishment of public schools and public libraries all over the land, thus helping to found two of America's proudest traditions.

One of the reasons for the Union's publishing Sunday-school songbooks was to illustrate in song its lesson plans. The first ones (from 1828) carried no music; tunes were first included in 1859.

The Sunday-school songbooks started to roll off the presses in the late 1850s. Up to that time, and beyond, Sunday schools were designed for children; there were no classes for adults at the time. Most of the songs were not very childlike, and many of the early gospel songs, as they were later called, were first published here. With their pithy, catchy choruses, the Sunday-school songs often sound like campmeeting songs. An excellent example is *Jesus Loves Me,* by William B. Bradbury, a Baptist songwriter and compiler (probably the best composer of early gospel songs and of hymns for children) who included many of the genuine campmeeting songs in his collections. His *Jesus Loves Me* could easily pass for a campmeeting song, with its emphasis on Jesus and heaven and death. The chorus text is in the favorite campmeeting form, *aaab* (see Section d-1 of Part II), and the entire melody is pentatonic (see Section d-5 of Part II). No wonder it was accepted around the world!

b. The Second Branch: The Gospel Songs, and Later Choruses

The emergence of the gospel songs, which had indeed started in the mid-1800s while the campmeeting songs were still in their heyday, was to be expected when the songwriters of the period realized the importance of providing a congregation with songs it could readily sing and remember. The campmeeting song provided a model.

At first, the composed songs were so similar to the campmeeting songs that one has trouble telling them apart.

Among the composed hymns that closely resemble campmeeting spirituals (and some of which were sung as such by campmeeting crowds) are *Come, every soul by sin oppressed; My days are gliding swiftly by; Revive us again; Blessed be the name of the Lord;* and *We're marching to Zion.* Several of these have refrain-texts in the *aaab* or *aaba* form; others have mother-hymns. All are rousingly singable. (See also Section d-6 of Part II.)

The cynic will say the gospel songwriters latched on to a good thing when they saw it—and it is true that they and their publishers made big money from their output. In their hands the chorus became tamed; its text was integrated with the body of the hymn, its pattern was made to conform to the musical sentence, the words rhymed tidily, and the vocal range was reduced to easy bounds. But it was still a chorus, catchy, compact, memorable, and popular. The words of the gospel song turned often from emotional to sentimental, but always they declaimed a personal message, straight to the heart of the individual. The gospel songs achieved a degree of popularity seldom known before. Their continued usefulness and effectiveness is a tribute to the spirit of the campmeeting song, which inspired them.

At the end of the nineteenth and in the early years of the twentieth centuries, gospel songwriters, possibly taking another look at the continuing popularity of the camp-meeting choruses, issued a group of new choruses (without stanzas)—short, catchy, and memorable, although less spontaneous-sounding than the folk choruses.

Perhaps the best known of these later, composed choruses were *Into my heart* and *Let the beauty of Jesus be seen in me.*

c. The Third Branch: Campmeeting Spirituals in Twentieth-Century Hymnals

Fifty-two different campmeeting choruses and hymns have persisted into the twentieth century in Northern hymnals. Of these, twenty-eight were found in four or more hymnals each. Some of these are tunes only, with new or different words, and some are not, strictly speaking, campmeeting songs but folk hymns found very frequently in the early campmeeting collections.

Among the most persistent of the fifty-two are *Amazing Grace* (48); *Balm in Gilead;* "Beloved"; "Cleansing Fountain"; *Come, thou fount of every blessing; Come to Jesus* (47); *Come, ye sinners poor and needy* (27); *Glory, glory, hallelujah* (41); *I am bound for the promised land* (25); *I can, I will, I do believe* (38); "Loving-Kindness" (30); *On Jordan's stormy banks I stand* (17); "Pleading Savior" (21); and various hymns to the tune of "Home, Sweet Home." (Figures in parenthesis denote the number in Song Examples, Part V.)

d. The Fourth Branch: Serious Compositions Quoting Campmeeting Spirituals

There are listed in the Library of Congress twelve compositions of "serious" style, based on revival tunes.

One is a Sousa march, several are works entitled *Campmeeting* or *Revival,* but the ones that show the most sympathy with the campmeeting songs are the several items by Charles Ives.

His String Quartet, Third Symphony, Violin and Piano Sonatas No. 2 and No. 4 ("Children's Day at the Camp Meeting"), and the song "General Booth Enters Heaven," all quote revival and gospel songs, for which he had a great affection. (He included gospel songs in the same category as campmeeting spirituals.)

Ives was wrapped up in his own joyous philosophies of life, and one of his greatest loves was the substance of the music of—or rather, the *sound* of—common people. He seems to have been fascinated with the singing at campmeetings, no matter how out of tune and unstudied it might be—because he felt its substance was what made humankind important. In his reminiscences he writes of camp meetings:

I remember, when I was a boy—at the outdoor Camp Meeting services in Redding [Conn.], all the farmers, their families and field hands, for miles around, would come afoot or in their farm wagons. I remember how the great waves of sound used to come through the trees—when things like *Beulah Land, Woodworth, Nearer My God to Thee, The Shining Shore, Nettleton, In the Sweet Bye and Bye* and the like were sung by thousands of "let-out" souls. . . . There was power and exaltation in these great conclaves of sound from humanity.[1]

e. The Greenest Growth: The Contemporary Scene

1. The Recent Evangelical Upsurge

Beginning with the 1960s, there are several remarkable aspects of religious and secular life that reveal something of the spirit of the early camp meetings.

There has been a powerful surge of evangelical feeling abroad. A cover story in *Time* magazine, entitled "Back to That Old-Time Religion," depicted the new feelings, referred to the First and Second Great Awakenings, and asked a question: "Will Evangelicalism simply go on consoling people in the face of alienation and apocalyptical fear, a not inconsiderable mission? Or will it move toward a 'Third Great Awakening' that might help regenerate American life?"[2]

2. Pentecostal Singing and the Holiness Movement in the South

The Holiness movement in southern Appalachia today stresses singing, with hand-clapping and foot-stomping. "The pronounced beat and rhythm are contagious and create group rapport. The participant tends to lose his self-consciousness, and becomes highly suggestible to the central theme of the songs, sermons, and testimonies."[3]

In her book *Revival!,* Eleanor Dickinson tells of the meetings she has attended in Kentucky, Tennessee, and West Virginia among the evangelical and Pentecostal denominations. She tells of the trances, the speaking in tongues, the mourners' bench, the dancing. The list of hymns she heard sung includes many old campmeeting favorites: *When I can read my title clear, On Jordan's stormy banks I stand* (17), *O how I love Jesus* (39), *I am bound for the promised land* (25)—and a song entitled *We need a whole lot more of Jesus and a lot less rock and roll!* [4] Earlier, H. L. Mencken visited a camp meeting in Tennessee. In *The American Scene* he describes the same phenomena as does Dickinson.[5]

3. The Charismatic Movement

In the North, the charismatic movement has encouraged extemporaneous singing and spoken congregational responses such as "Praise to Jesus," "Thank you, Father," "Hosanna," and "Hallelujah." In what would have been called a "protracted meeting" in the nineteenth century, forty thousand people met in July, 1977, in Kansas City, in what was hailed as the greatest gathering of Christians in eight hundred years. A newspaper report told of the "emotional and ecstatic experience." "Singing in the Spirit" was part of the excitement.[6]

4. Congregational Participation in the Roman Catholic Church

Today's Roman Catholic Church has experienced a great change inspired by Vatican II. Congregational participation has in many churches become lively. The pamphlet *Music in Catholic Worship* gives directives for such participation:

Music should assist the assembled believers to express and share the gift of faith that is within them. . . . The quality of joy and enthusiasm which music adds to community worship cannot be gained in any other way. . . .

The acclamations are shouts of joy which arise from the whole assembly. . . . It is of their nature that they be rhythmically strong, melodically appealing, and affirmative.[7]

Among the informal publications of the Catholics are the *Monthly Missalettes*.[8] Each contains a limited selection of Negro and white spirituals: *Amazing Grace* (48), *Pleading Savior* (21), and so forth, some with words more appropriate for Catholics. One finds *On Jordan's stormy banks* (17), with the chorus *I am bound for the promised land* (25). (Figures in parentheses indicate the numbers of the Song Examples in Part V.)

A number of "contemporary folk hymns" with choruses are given. Other choruses old and new are included. Several recent Catholic hymnals, including *Worship II* (1975) and *The Catholic Hymnal* (1974), also reflect the old-new spirit in their inclusion of spirituals and choruses.

The list of folk hymns and choruses in these books and pamphlets seems limited; the same ones are repeated over and over. But the evangelical spirit has arisen in a new place!

5. Contemporary "Folk" Hymns

In the Protestant church, some of today's worshipers are clapping their hands, snapping their fingers, and singing

Glory, Hallelujah! Beginning in the 1960s, a new informal type of hymnody developed which bears close resemblance in some respects to the campmeeting songs. Like them, the "contemporary folk hymns" (which are, strictly speaking, not folk music at all, but have appropriated the popular folk elements) were the result of rebellion against the hymnodic establishment. Their language is fresh, realistic, secular, and sometimes raw; they have abandoned standard meters and forms; they frequently use the ballad style and the leader-response and secular rhythms stressing syncopation. In the campmeeting spirit, they have discovered joy, celebration, dance, and laughter.[9]

In *Genesis,* typical of many recent informal songbooks, there are twenty-eight items that reflect the campmeeting spirit.[10] One is in leader-response form, one is an independent chorus, two have ejaculatory choruses (*Alleluia,* and—up-to-date—*Hip hooray*).

6. A "Happening"

As a modern secular phenomenon closely parallel to the campmeeting experience, one might choose the "happening" at Woodstock, 1969. This was a mammoth concert of rock music, which, like the early camp meetings, attracted more people and generated more rapture than anything else of its time. The young men who conceived of the idea, organized it, and financed it, told their story in a book, *Young Men with Unlimited Capital.* Here is an excerpt; even the rhapsodic language reminds one of the camp meetings!

"This is the largest crowd of people ever assembled for a concert in the history of the world. . . . But it's so dark out there we can't see you and you can't see each other. So when I say 'three' I want every one of you to light a match. O.K.? . . . One . . . two . . . THREE!"

And there was an elevation of the host, a crescent transubstantiation of darkness into light, a glow neither celestial nor infernal, but human, achingly, beautifully human, human almost to the point of tears. . . .

"I wanna take you higher . . . " Sly chanted, and the crowd answered him "Higher!!!" again and again, each time from a more rarefied eminence, until height and depth lost meaning and there was only the moment, the eternally transient Now of existence suffusing the mingled thousands with a sense of fruition, of communion, and of reward.[11]

7. A Re-incarnation of the Campmeeting Chorus?

And finally, as we look at the contemporary secular flowering of the campmeeting spirit, here is an example that may not be quite so flippant as it first appears. In this age of secularization, are not the singing commercials something like the campmeeting songs? They are short, they are catchy, they are easily learned, and forgotten (alas) with difficulty.

They are repetitive; they are even ecstatic. They sell something—the materially good life—which may characterize our generation as surely as yearning for heaven characterized the nineteenth century. Is it too cynical to nominate them for the present-day re-incarnation of a 180-year-old phenomenon?

Yes, the ecstasy that surged to the point of hysteria in the camp meetings is with us still, in new and varied guises. It finds perhaps its best expression in song. Who can tell when and where and how a strong new branch of the tree will burgeon on the trunk that started growing prodigiously a hundred and eighty years ago?

Part V. Song Examples

a. Forty-eight Annotated Northern
Campmeeting Spirituals
Used as Illustrations of the Text

No. 1. "I Can't Stay Away" *Practical Church Music* (1909), 100

I Can't Stay Away. This haunting spiritual presents an illustration of most of the elements of the camp-meeting song. (See Section d of Part II.) The combination of words and tune was not found anywhere else than in Lorenz's *Practical Church Music,*[1] where the writer says of it: "Less than thirty years ago I heard the following 'spiritual' still sung spontaneously in southern Ohio. It has the genuine pentatonal characteristics which mark aboriginal music. . . . The effect was very powerful; it had great dignity as well as force." In *Spiritual Folk-Songs of Early America,*[2] Jackson presents a wide variant of this tune, found in Cooper's 1902 edition of *Sacred Harp;* the words of the interrupting refrain are the same, but the mother-hymn is different. The early book of Negro spirituals, Allen's *Slave Songs of the United States,*[3] gives a spiritual, *I can't stay behind,* the text form of which is like *I can't stay away (aaba),* but its music is major and does not resemble this white spiritual.

87

O that will be joyful is an exceptionally popular chorus, found in forty-seven instances in this study, only one of which was Southern. It is usually associated with *How pleasant thus to dwell below,* but there are no fewer than thirteen different mother-hymns used with this chorus and tune. The chorus—words and music—is retained in the parody, *The man who has plenty of good peanuts.* Note the text extension of lines three and four of the hymn. Like many other campmeeting choruses, this is a favorite with the Pennsylvania Dutch at their "bushmeetings."[4]

No. 3. "We're Marching Through Immanuel's Ground"   *Sacred Melodies for Social Worship* (1859), 292
(Original in F)

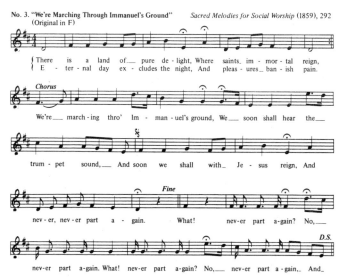

The chorus of this song was found in twenty books of this study, from 1846 to a twentieth-century Salvation Army songbook, with a variety of mother-hymns. This is an unusually long song for campmeeting use, but it is repetitive and catchy, and was sung at the very popular farewell services. Is there a relationship (beyond coincidence) between this chorus and the Gilbert and Sullivan refrain "What, never? no, never!"? (Can you imagine W. S. Gilbert attending a camp meeting?)

89

No. 4. "Pilgrim's Farewell" *The Christian Lyre* (1837), 38 (Excerpts)

Fare - well, fare - well, Fare - well, my lov - ing friends, fare -well.

I'll____ march to Ca -naan's land, I'll__ land on Ca -naan's shore,

This comparatively long song of parting is one of the oldest songs in campmeeting style, first appearing in *The Psalmodist's Companion,* 1793, before the actual beginning of the camp meetings. It is found in twenty-one books of this study, from *Christian Harmony,* 1805 (with different words), to the *Primitive Baptist Hymnal,* 1879. It is listed among the Eighty Most Popular Tunes in *White Spirituals of the Southern Uplands,*[5] and is sung by the Western Wind Vocal Ensemble on their record *Early American Vocal Music* (Nonesuch 71276).

No. 5. "And We'll March Around Jerusalem" *The Revivalist* (1872), 358

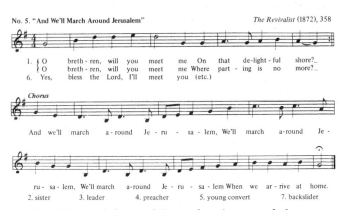

1. { O breth - ren, will you meet me On that de-light - ful shore?_
   { O breth - ren, will you meet me Where part - ing is no more?_
6. Yes, bless the Lord, I'll meet you (etc.)

And we'll march a - round Je - ru - sa - lem, We'll march a-round Je -

ru - sa - lem, We'll march a-round Je - ru - sa - lem When we ar - rive at home.

2. sister   3. leader   4. preacher   5. young convert   7. backslider

And we'll march around Jerusalem is one of the songs associated with the farewell service at camp meetings, when all those present marched around camp, shaking hands and singing. Note the wide range, also the "family word." Verse 6 may have been used throughout the song as a response; one can imagine the women responding to verse 2, the leaders to verse 3, and so forth. But what about the backsliders, after verse 7?

This tune, usually known as "Invitation," was first published in 1805 in *The Christian Harmony,* compiled by singing-school master Jeremiah Ingalls. It may have been a folk melody, or it may have been written by Ingalls in folk style.[6] In subsequent appearances, the opening rhythm is sometimes a dotted eighth and sixteenth. Another hymn frequently sung to this tune is *Come, ye sinners poor and needy.* The tune was popular for a hundred years.

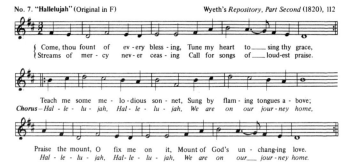

Come, thou fount of ev-ery bless-ing, Tune my heart to____ sing thy grace,
Streams of mer-cy nev-er ceas-ing Call for songs of____ loud-est praise.

Teach me some me-lo-dious son-net, Sung by flam-ing tongues a-bove;
Chorus—Hal-le-lu-jah, Hal-le-lu-jah, We are on our jour-ney home,

Praise the mount, O fix me on it, Mount of God's un-chang-ing love.
Hal-le-lu-jah, Hal-le-lu-jah, We are on our____ jour-ney home.

This is the first published version of the tune which is the basis of present-day "Nettleton." The words of the chorus illustrate the often-found *non sequitur* that campmeeting singers would attach to a favorite hymn.

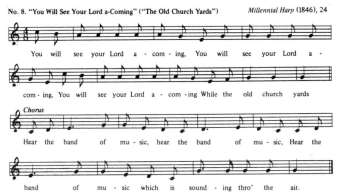

You will see your Lord a - com - ing, You will see your Lord a - com - ing, You will see your Lord a - com - ing While the old church yards

Chorus

Hear the band of mu - sic, hear the band of mu - sic, Hear the band of mu - sic which is sound - ing thro' the air.

This spirited song of the Second Coming has as its tune "The Old Granite State," a song sung by the famous Singing Hutchinson Family of New Hampshire. It is said that the Adventists used to gather in cemeteries to sing this song. It was published chiefly in Adventist songbooks from 1842 on, including *The Millennial Harp* and *The Jubilee Harp*. There were ten one-line verses, such as *He'll bring his Father with him, Hear Gabriel blow his trumpet, He'll waken all the nations,* and *There'll be a mighty wailing.* The text form is *aaab*.

Chorus

Chorus 1 – O there will be mourn - ing, mourn - ing, mourn - ing, mourn - ing,
Chorus 2 – " " " " glo - ry, (etc.)
Chorus 3 – " " " " shout - ing, (etc.)

O there will be mourn - ing At the judg - ment seat __ of Christ.
glo - ry
shout - ing

1. Par -ents and chil - dren there will part, Par - ents and chil - dren there will part,
2. Wives and hus - bands there will part, (etc.)
3. Broth-ers and sis - ters there will part, (etc.)

Par -ents and chil - dren there will part, Will part to meet_ no more.

4. Friends and neighbors   5. Pastors and people   6. Saints and angels there will meet.

The words first appeared in 1835, the tune in 1837. *O there will be mourning* is a good example of the many songs about the Last Judgment, a popular topic when almost all denominations were millennialist. It could be—and often was—lengthened by spontaneous addition of "family word" verses. There is a Negro version. Note that the chorus comes first.

No. 10. "The Last Trumpet" (Original in G Minor)   *Evangelical Harp* (1845), 40

O get your hearts in or - der,   or - der,   or - der, O get your hearts in

Chorus

or - der for the end of time, For Ga-briel's go-ing to blow,_ by and

by, by and by, For__ Ga-briel's go-ing to blow_ by and by. _____

O get your hearts in order is an example of the one-line campmeeting hymn, with chorus. Many of these millennial hymns, popular in most denominations at the time, had a succession of short phrases describing the Last Judgment. The tune is modal (Aeolian, or natural minor).

No. 11. "O Tell Me No More"

The Revivalist (1872), 332
"As sung by Rev. A. C. Rose"

O_____ tell me no more Of_____ this world's vain __ store,

The time __ for such__ tri - fles with ____ me now is ____ o'er.

This version of the song shows the melodic effects of oral transmission, with its many holds and passing notes. The triplets may represent a pitchless slide on the part of the singer. The oldest recording of this tune dates from 1805; the latest in this study was 1894.

1. What ship is this that is pass - ing__ by? O__ glo - ry, hal - le -

lu - jah! Why, it's old ship Zi - on, hal - le -

lu - jah! Why, it's old ship Zi - on, hal - le - lu - jah.

2. O who is your captain and what is his name?
   'Tis the meek and lowly Jesus.

Seven stanzas are given, each with question and answer, in the popular dialogue form. The figure of a ship with Christ as captain appears in several songs. The first appearance found with both tune and words was in 1845; the latest was 1889 in a songbook of the South, where the song was very popular. The words and music are paralleled in a Negro spiritual.

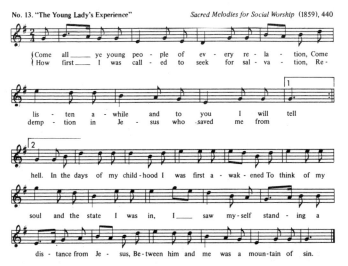

The ballad was a favorite of campmeeting goers, especially when it told the personal experience of the convert. Many ballads opened with the phrase *Come all ye,* and that phrase became a nickname for that type of song. *The Young Lady's Experience* is a typical campmeeting come-all-ye, relating how the young lady was saved from her sin. The tune has all the elements of a folk song, with its five-toned melody (the one F# is a passing tone) and its wide range. This song was not found elsewhere.

I have some friends be - fore me gone,
I'm re - solved to trav - el on,
Glo - ry, hal - le - lu - jah! And

Glo - ry, hal - le - lu - jah! We'll go on, trav - el on, Glo - ry, hal - le -

lu - jah! We'll go on, trav - el on, O glo - ry, hal - le - lu - jah!

Note the use of the Aeolian mode; the tune sometimes occurs as Dorian, with B-naturals at the x's above. This song is a good example of the interrupting refrain, occurring not only in the verse but in the chorus also. The Southern version of this chorus, *Shout on, we're gaining ground,* is thought to be one of the earliest of the choruses, perhaps originating in the eighteenth century.[7]

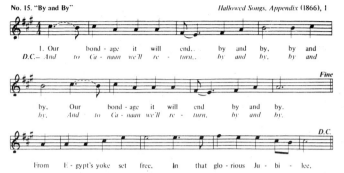

This beautiful hymn-text was found twelve times in the present study, always with the by-and-by refrain but with six entirely different tunes! Half of the occurrences were in Southern books; the dates run from 1846 to 1913. Note that the text-form is like that of *Wondrous Love*. The Adventist books and two others used the hymn *We shall see a light appear* with the by-and-by refrain and *Ride on, Jesus* as the chorus.

There   is ___ a ___ heav'n ___ o'er   yon - der   skies,
A   heav'n_ where_ pleas - ure_ ___ nev - er   dies,

A   heav'n I   some - time hope_ to   see,
But fear a - gain___ 'tis not ___ for me.

Chorus
But   Je - sus,_ Je - sus   is   my friend, O   hal - le - lu - jah,

hal - le - lu - jah,   Je - sus, Je - sus   is___   my   friend.

Jesus Is My Friend, with its very free, fluid melody (note the three-measure phrases) and Aeolian modality, is surely one of the most beautiful of all folk hymns. The freedom of the form reflects the oral tradition found in *Sacred Melodies for Social Worship* and *The Revivalist;* in *Devotional Melodies,* however, the tune was sadly altered by its arranger. The words alone are also found in nine songsters.

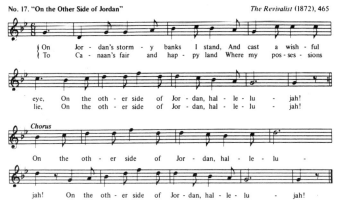

On Jordan's stormy banks I stand is one of the very most popular hymns of campmeeting times. It was set to many different tunes and attracted many different choruses, both in the North and in the South. Here, the interrupting refrain appears after the hymn's second and fourth lines, and again twice as the chorus. The tune is in the Aeolian mode, and somewhat resembles the Civil War song *When Johnny Comes Marching Home.* There are also Negro spiritual parallels.

This song furnishes one of the best examples of a mother-hymn (*Show pity, Lord* is one of the most popular) with an interrupting refrain *(Save, mighty Lord),* and a chorus that repeats the refrain. The B-natural makes the tune an especially clear example of the Dorian mode. This particular version of the song was found in the North from 1853 to 1909.

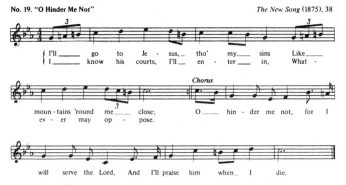

The words of this song were found in five songsters dating from 1830, and the tune in only two books, the other (1879) with a different mother-hymn. The text is based on Genesis 24:56. A Dorian flavor is given by the A-natural in the chorus. It is possible that the triplets represent the slides of oral transmission. The title phrase is also found in a Negro spiritual.

No. 20. "The Lord Is Merciful"   *The Revivalist* (1872), 147

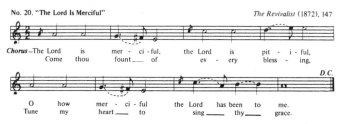

In this short song the chorus comes first. The mother-hymn is just one line, not even the usual rhymed couplet! Note that the extra syllables of the chorus are taken care of through grace notes. The sharp on F puts this into the Dorian mode.

Hallowed Songs (1866), 56

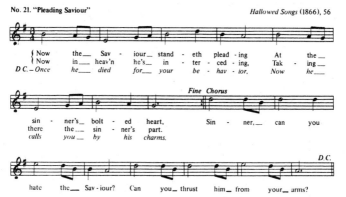

This very popular campmeeting hymn is still in use today, in the South, the North, and even in England. One can find several different versions of the rhythm, as for instance a 2/4 measure opening with a dotted quarter and two sixteenths, but the shape of the melody is usually the same, and it is almost always five-toned, with the fourth and seventh tones missing.

Note the use of "Hallelujah" as an interjection, four times per stanza. The interrupting refrain (which really interrupts the meaning of the mother-hymn couplet) is repeated for the chorus, giving the song an unusual unity. The tune may be interpreted as being in the Mixolydian mode (DEF# GABCD). This song was found in no other campmeeting songbooks besides *Sacred Melodies for Social Worship*.

The opening couplet of this song-text is found in a large number of campmeeting spirituals. This one and many others like it were used as two-line verses with little thought to their meaning. Notice that the interrupting refrain is extended into the chorus. Indeed, the phrase "We'll be there" is sung six times in each verse!

One finds strong parallels in Negro music with both words and music of this song. Note the close resemblance of the chorus tune to the second half of version b of *Amazing Grace* (No. 48). The sharp on G was probably added by the editor, thus turning an Aeolian tune into minor.

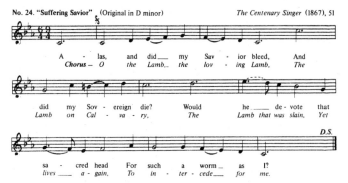

A - las, and did___ my Sav - ior bleed, And
Chorus — O the Lamb,_ the lov - ing Lamb, The

did my Sov - ereign die? Would he ___ de - vote that
Lamb on Cal - va - ry, The Lamb that was slain, Yet

sa - cred head For such a worm __ as I?
lives ___ a - gain, To in - ter - cede___ for me.

Dating to the beginning of the century, the chorus *O the Lamb, the loving Lamb* is found frequently in the campmeeting collections, with a variety of tunes as well as of mother-hymns. The favorite mother-hymn is *Alas, and did my Savior bleed;* "Suffering Savior" is the favorite tune, repeated for the chorus. It is also found from 1838 as an independent chorus. The natural on B should have been omitted; with B-flat the tune is in the Aeolian (natural minor) mode, as in the Southern songbooks. There are variations in the many occurrences: the appearance in *Revival Hymns,* 1842, is in 4/4 time.

I am bound for the promised land is a memorable tune sung in either major or minor. (Minor predominates in the Southern books, major in the Northern.) *On Jordan's stormy banks I stand* is the favorite mother-hymn, with *O joyful sound of gospel grace* a strong second. The tune is being used in twentieth-century hymnals. Jackson, in *Spiritual Folk Songs of Early America,* calls it "an enormously well-liked spiritual" and points out its resemblance to an English morris dance.[8] The text-form of the chorus is *aaba.*

I want to wear the crown is one of the campmeeting songs that appeared in several of the early songbooks, in the 1840s. Here we have a favorite mother-hymn, a chorus text in *aaab* form, and an interrupting refrain *(I want to wear the crown)*. Several of the appearances in other songbooks are in the minor.

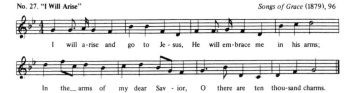

I will arise is an Aeolian chorus. (The editors of *The Revivalist* and other songbooks have "minorized" it by sharping the seventh.) It is often used with *Come, ye sinners poor and needy* or *Come, thou fount of every blessing,* but frequently as an independent chorus. Found from 1811 in Southern hymnbooks, its first appearance in the North seems to have been in *The Revivalist,* 1868. Strangely enough, of the twenty-two occurrences found in the present study, nine come from twentieth-century hymnals. It deserves its increasing popularity. There are Negro-spiritual parallels.

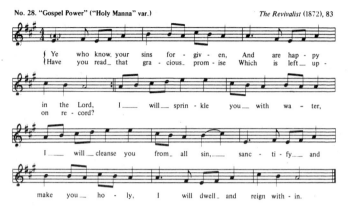

Ye who know your sins for - giv - en, And are hap - py
Have you read_ that gra - cious_ prom - ise Which is left_ up -

in the Lord, I____ will___ sprin - kle you___ with wa - ter,
on re - cord?

I____ will ___ cleanse you from_ all sin,___ sanc - ti - fy___ and

make you__ ho - ly, I will dwell_ and reign with - in.

This is a Northern variation of a very popular tune, "Holy Manna." Here the words reflect the Holiness movement. Notice the running notes in the fifth and seventh measures: these are a variant from the most commonly known version. This tune, with the Holy Manna words, is found today in some of the new-style hymnals and songbooks. "Holy Manna" is present in the Negro-spiritual tradition as well as white. It is basically five-toned, with added passing D's.

"Pisgah" is one of the Eighty Most Popular Tunes in Jackson's *White Spirituals the Southern Uplands.*[9] It is found in the Robert Shaw Chorale recording *Sing to the Lord,* and is a favorite in both Northern and Southern songbooks. The present study revealed ten different hymns set to the tune, many with choruses repeating the tune. In this particular appearance, the chorus takes the form of a text-extension. The melody is five-toned and sounds like a dance tune. Compare it to No. 30—the melodies open very similarly.

A - wake, my soul, in joy - ful lays, And sing thy great Re -
deem - er's praise; He just - ly claims a song from me; His
lov - ing - kind - ness, O how free! His lov - ing - kind - ness,
lov - ing - kind - ness, His lov - ing - kind - ness, O how free!

By far the most popular of the Northern campmeeting hymns, with eighty-nine appearances in the songbooks of this study, *Loving-Kindness* raises some puzzling questions. It is a standard hymn text that, with few and minor exceptions, is never varied either in text or music. This is almost unheard of in folk hymns, no two appearances of which are (in general) ever identical. Moreover, it has an extended refrain instead of a chorus, and the extended refrain is not exclusively a campmeeting-song form. (The fourth line of each stanza is here extended in a four-measure refrain.)

On the the other hand, the tune is a rollicking one that strongly suggests an origin as a dance tune, quite in the tradition of "Pisgah" and "Canaan." Also, the tune is frequently credited as a "Western Air," which generally means it is of campmeeting origin. Compare the tune to No. 29.

Thus the questions remain. What is its source? Why are there almost never any variations in text or music?

Lute of Zion (1853), 285

This is and was a very popular tune, found sixty times in the books of the present study. The chorus words, "O Canaan, bright Canaan," seldom vary, except for the alternate *sweet Canaan*, but a great number of different mother-hymns are used. It is as popular in the South as in the North, but the Southern tune is a wide variant of the Northern one, which is perhaps the more distinctive. Notice the interrupting refrain, which occurs not only between the mother-hymn couplet lines but also at the end of the chorus. Note also the wide range.

Will you go is the interrupting refrain used most frequently in the songbooks of this study. There are eleven different mother-hymns used with it, but the one given above is the overwhelming favorite, occurring sixty-seven times. There is no chorus. This song occurred from 1842 to 1909, in South and North.

Jesus, my all was one of the universally loved hymns of the first half of the nineteenth century. Here its first couplet is used as a mother-hymn, to which is attached an interrupting refrain and a chorus of unusual unity of theme. The song was found in Baptist, Methodist, and Adventist books of the 1840s.

We have but the one more river to cross has textual parallels with Negro and Southern white spirituals. The tune is five-toned, but in a different pattern from the usual pentatonic; here it is the fourth and sixth degrees of the scale that are missing, not the usual fourth and seventh. The words are an excellent example of the interrupting refrain, and the chorus repeats the music of the verse.

No. 35. "O Hallelujah"   *The Revivalist* (1872), 334

O tell me no more Of this world's vain store. The

Chorus — O   hal - le - lu - jah,   O   hal - le - lu - jah,   O

time for such tri - fles With me now is o'er.

hal - le–,   O   hal - le–,   O   hal - le - lu - jah!

The mother-hymn used here is one of the most popular; it reflects the world-rejection so prevalent at the time of the Great Awakening. The use of *halle-* and *hallelujah* is notable. The music of the chorus repeats that of the verse.

No. 36. "Glory to the Lamb" (Original in F)*

B. W. Gorham
Campmeeting Manual (1854) p. ix

Chorus— Glo - ry to the Lamb,_____ Glo - ry to the

Lamb,_____ Glo - ry to the__ Lamb._____ 1. The

world is o - ver - come_____ by the blood of__ the Lamb.

Glo - ry to the Lamb, ____ Glo - ry to the Lamb._____

* Rhythmic notation altered

Glory to the Lamb is not a folk hymn; it appeared first in a campmeeting manual written by the preacher who wrote the words and music, in 1854. It was widely used after that, and one can imagine the crowds singing this solemn melody, which suggests a Gregorian chant. The appearance in *The Revivalist* has the chorus following the verse. Don Yoder remembers hearing it at an Evangelical United Brethren campmeeting in 1955, sung in German, with thrilling effect.[10]

Chorus— And O I will go, and O____ I will go, And O I will
go ____ in - to yon bright world.   1. There we'll sing and shout with the an - gels,
Shout with the an - gels, shout with the an - gels,   in that con - gre - ga - tion.

3. There we'll walk and talk with Jesus   7. O brother –
5. O father, will you meet me?   8. O sister –
6. O mother, will you meet me?   10. O mourner – (etc.)

And O I will go is a spirited song that was found nowhere except in *Devotional Melodies,* except that the words are in *The Chorus,* 1858. *Devotional Melodies* gives eleven verses. Note that the chorus is placed first, with the verses following. The text-form is *aaab;* there is a nice use of the "family word," necessitating the omission of extra notes in the melody.

I can, I will, I do be - lieve, I can, I will,__ I do be - lieve, I
can, and I will, and I do be - lieve That Je - sus died__ for me._____

This popular and rousing chorus may be used either as an independent chorus, or as a chorus attached to any of a variety of mother-hymns, chiefly *I'm kneeling at the mercy-seat. Pentecostal Hymns No. 1* lists four mother-hymns that may be used, including *Just as I am* and *Father, I stretch my hands to thee.* The earliest appearance in this study is 1859; the most recent is 1961. Another chorus with parallel text is *I will believe, I do believe.* A very similar tune is found in *The Revivalist* with the words *Jesus is the bleeding Lamb* (3x) *That was slain.* the text-form for all these is *aaab.*

No. 39. "O How I Love Jesus"   *The Revivalist* (1872), 456 (Chorus only)

This chorus, attached to various mother-hymns, was found forty-two times in the present study, but never earlier than 1868; ten of the appearances were in twentieth-century songbooks. The tune was popular with the blacks. It is part of a tune family of four campmeeting songs, all in 6/8 and with similar melodic outlines and dancelike movement. The text-form is *aaab*.

No. 40. "O Brother, Be Faithful" (Original in F)   *The Revivalist* (1872), 433

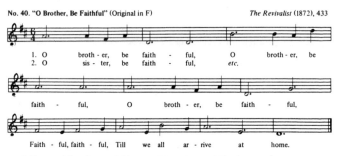

3. There we shall see Jesus.   4. There we will shout glory.   5. There'll be no more parting.

Here we have the one-line verse form, which, extended extemporaneously, can be prolonged almost endlessly. The text-form is *aaab*. Another Northern variant is the early *I'll try to prove faithful*, found in the 1805 tunebook *The Christian Harmony*.

O brother, be faithful has a close Negro variant, *Lord, make me more patient*.

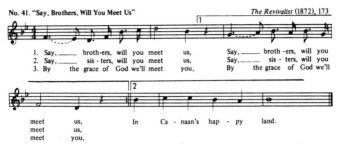

1. Say,_____ broth-ers, will you meet   us,   Say,_____ broth -ers, will you
2. Say,_____ sis - ters, will you meet   us,   Say,_____ sis - ters, will you
3. By   the grace of God we'll meet   you,   By   the grace of God we'll

meet   us,   In   Ca - naan's hap - py   land.
meet   us,
meet   you,

Say, brothers, will you meet us illustrates the singability of
the campmeeting choruses; it is the campmeeting chorus
most often parodied, from the time of its first creation up to
the present. (See Section f of Part II.) L. A. Banks relates
its story in his *Immortal Songs of Camp and Field*.[11] His first
meeting with the song was in Charleston in 1859, with a
performance soon after at the YMCA of Albany, N.Y.
(But the present study reveals a publication in *Songs of
Zion,* 1851.) Banks says, "It has been claimed that the
Millerites [Adventists] used the tune to a hymn, 'We'll see
the angels coming through the old church yard (3 times) /
Shouting through the air / Glory, glory, hallelujah.' " (See
Song No. 8.)

The word "sisters" in verse two suggests the "family
word"; the third verse suggests a dialogue effect.

The Battle Hymn of the Republic employs the tune for the
verse, with many extra syllables, and for the chorus in the
original form.

There are several different sets of religious words used
with the tune: *Now I know what makes me happy, When
this poor body lies a-mouldering in the grave,* and several
variants on the *Say, brother* theme. Mother-hymns include
Ye soldiers of the cross, arise, O when shall I see Jesus, and
On Jordan's stormy banks I stand. The tune has Negro
parallels; the text is in *aaab* form.

No. 42. "Give Me Jesus" (Rhythm altered)   *The Revivalist* (1872), 89

1. When I'm hap - py, hear me sing, When I'm hap - py, hear me sing,
2. When in sor - row, hear me pray, When in sor - row, hear me pray,

Give me Je - sus. Give me Je - sus,_____ give me Je - sus,_____

You may have all the world, Give me Je - sus._____

3. When I'm dying, hear me cry.   4. When I'm rising, hear me shout.

Give me Jesus is found with quite similar words and tune in both black and white versions, and seems to be a favorite with each culture. In this version, the text-form of the verse is the often used *aaab,* while the chorus is *aaba.* There are five one-line stanzas.

This is one of the most expressive of the American folk hymns.

122

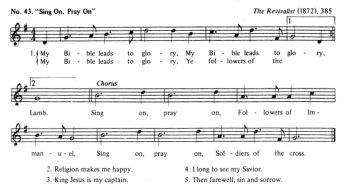

1. My Bi - ble leads to glo - ry, My Bi - ble leads to glo - ry,
   My Bi - ble leads to glo - ry, Ye fol - lowers of the

Lamb. Sing on, pray on, Fol - lowers of Im -

man - u - el, Sing on, pray on, Sol - diers of the cross.

2. Religion makes me happy.   4. I long to see my Savior.
3. King Jesus is my captain.   5. Then farewell, sin and sorrow.

There are seven one-line verses; the verses have no
particular unity of thought. The text-form of the verse is
aaab. There is a closely related Shaker song, with a minor
tune, and the words as follow:

"Oh brethren, ain't you happy (3 times)
Ye followers of the Lamb.

Sing on, dance on, followers of Emmanuel. . . ."[12]
There are few instances in which Shaker songs are derived
so clearly from campmeeting songs as this one.

123

Where,   O   where   are ' the   He - brew   chil - dren,   Where,   O
Chorus—By   and   by   we'll go   home   to   meet   them,   By   and

where   are   the   He - brew   chil - dren,   Where,   O   where   are   the
by   we'll   go   home   to   meet   them,   By   and   by   we'll   go

He - brew   chil - dren?   Safe   now   in   the   prom - ised   land.
home   to   meet   them.   Safe   now   in   the   prom - ised   land.

2. good Elijah	4. prophet Daniel	6. martyred Stephen
3. good old Moses	5. weeping Mary	7. blessed Jesus

This song is found all over the land, in the North, in the South, among whites, among blacks. It is the subject of many parodies, including *Where, O where is pretty little Susie*[13] and the college song *Where, O where are the verdant freshmen.*

Successive verses celebrate various biblical characters almost endlessly. Some versions begin with "the righteous Noah"; the title is sometimes given as "Ancient Worthies." The text-form of most versions is *aaab.* The spiritual is included in one of the Robert Shaw Chorale records.

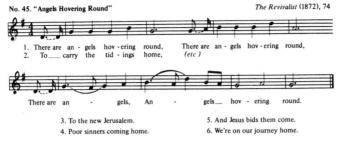

1. There are an - gels hov -ering round, There are an - gels hov -ering round,
2. To__ carry the tid - ings home, *(etc)*

There are an - gels, An - gels__ hov - ering round.

3. To the new Jerusalem.   5. And Jesus bids them come.
4. Poor sinners coming home.   6. We're on our journey home.

Angels Hovering is one of the favorite independent choruses, with up to thirteen one-line verses, which build up in meaning as the tune progresses. In *Songs of Praises*, 1886, the music is written as a chant—surely a unique example in campmeeting recording! *The Wesleyan Psalmist* notes about this song, "How often has this short tune inspired the whole company when sinners were turning to the Lord or Christians were rejoicing!" There are, in true folk-tune style, minor variations of the tune from book to book.

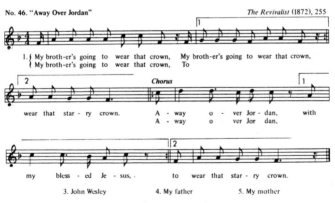

1. { My broth-er's going to wear that crown, My broth-er's going to wear that crown,
   { My broth-er's going to wear that crown, To

wear that star - ry crown.   A - way   o - ver Jor-dan,   with
                                  A - way   o   ver Jor-dan,

my   bless - ed Je - sus, .   to   wear that star - ry crown.

3. John Wesley   4. My father   5. My mother

This song, sometimes called the "clapping song," [14] has one-line stanzas featuring the "family word." "Away over Jordan" was an ubiquitous phrase found in Northern, Southern, and Negro spirituals.

No. 47a. "Come to Jesus"   *The Revivalist* (1872), 142

1. Come to Je - sus, come to Je - sus, Come to Je - sus just now,   Just
2. He will save you, he will save you, He will save you just now,   Just

now   come   to   Je - sus,   Come   to   Je - sus   just   now.
now   he   will   save   you,   He   will save   you   just   now.

No. 47b. "Come to Jesus" (Original in B♭)   *The Christian Lyre* (1837), 73

Come to Je - sus, Come and wel-come, come and wel-come, come and wel-come, come.

Come to Je - sus, Come and wel-come, come and wel-come, come and wel-come, come.

Come   and   wel - come,   sin - ner,   come.

There are three different tunes for this all-time favorite among campmeeting choruses.

The one appearing in *The Revivalist* was by far the most widely used. There are minor variants; the most common begins *do-re-do*. The earliest appearance found for this tune was 1851 (*Songs of Zion*). Up to nineteen verses are given, sometimes with Scripture references. There is a Negro version, *Sanctofy Me [sic]*. The *Revivalist* version is the subject of much parodying. *Clementine* and *Found a Peanut* (or *Horseshoe*) are the best known.

The second version here is the earliest and least popular; it is complicated (sounding something like an auctioneer's call) and did not persist long. It was found in only one other book, *Jubilee Harp,* 1868, and is given here because of its early appearance in *The Christian Lyre.*

The version omitted here is not interesting musically; it first appeared in 1842 in *Revival Hymns* with thirty verses! This version is also found in the first collection of Negro spirituals, *Slave Songs of the United States,* 1867.

The Adventists liked *Come to Jesus,* adapting the verses to their own needs.

No. 48a. "Amazing Grace" ("Harmony Grove") (Original in A)   Tune from *Virginia Harmony* (1836), 17

A - maz - ing ___ grace! how sweet the sound That ___ saved a ___ wretch like ___ me: I once was ___ lost, but ___ now am found, Was ___ blind, but ___ now I see.

No. 48b. "Amazing Grace" (Original in A Minor)   *Sacred Melodies for Social Worship* (1859), 333

A - maz - ing grace! how sweet the sound That saved a wretch like me:
I ___ once was lost, ___ but now am found, Was blind, but now I see.

'Twas grace that taught my heart to ___ fear, And ___ grace my ___ fears re - lieved;

How ___ pre - cious did that grace ap - pear ___ The hour I first be - lieved.

Amazing Grace is popular today, and it was popular in the time of the camp meetings and revival meetings. Two settings are given here, and two others were found, all folk melodies. The one we know best shows the influence of oral transmission in its ornamental notes, as does the second in its holds. Both have "gapped" scales; the second is in the Aeolian mode. The tune of the second is a variant of the folk hymn tune "Fiducia," found in Southern tunebooks.

A twentieth-century author wrote, "At times the combination of words and music made a perfect unit and got fixed enough in the ear of the pioneer to bring nostalgia to the aid of faith. A case in point was *Amazing Grace,* which lost none of its force, no matter how often it was repeated. . . . Sung by a great crowd of people it could melt the hardest heart and the rocks around to boot." [15]

b. Index of the Hymns, Choruses, Refrains, and Tunes

* = Chorus
+ = Refrain

Tune Names are in quotation marks.

(Many of the choruses begin with *And* or *O* and should be looked for under these words.)

128

SONG EXAMPLES

GLORY, HALLELUJAH!

An Explanation of Terms

Terminology in this field is neither complete nor consistent; hence, the following terms have been coined, adapted, or adopted for this study. An asterisk indicates a special use, not as conventionally defined.

Camp Meeting: a form of country revival meeting originating on the Western frontier in 1800, soon widespread; held in forest groves, with tents for lodging.

*Campmeeting hymn: a "standard" hymn-text, without chorus; already known to campmeeting attendants, and set to a presumably familiar folk tune.

Campmeeting spiritual: informal hymn often with refrain and chorus, taking form in camp and revival meetings.

*Chorus: short, informal, folk-created addition to a hymn, often spontaneously attached to a "standard" hymn (in part or whole); often containing ejaculations or "shouting words".

*Extension refrain: an extension of the stanzas, in turn.

Family word: the opening word (brother, sister, preacher, sinner, etc.) of successive verses of many campmeeting spirituals, by the use of which new verses are created without any other change of wording.

*Folk hymn: a sacred song "originating among the common people and characterized by a traditional oral transmission and usually anonymous authorship." (Definition adapted from *American Heritage Dictionary.*)

Gapped scales: scales of fewer than seven tones. Most common: pentatonic (five-toned), omitting the fourth and seventh steps of the major scale.

*Gathering note: an extended note at the beginning of a phrase, especially the first phrase of a song, to help singers assemble their forces for attacking the music.

Hymn: a corporate song of praise to God; designating either words only, or both words and tune.

Hymnal: a book of words and tunes, usually for a specific denomination.

Hymnbook: a book of hymn-texts without music. (See "Songster," below.)

*Independent chorus: a short (or extended) folk-created chorus not attached to a mother-hymn.

*Interrupting refrain: a folk-created refrain interpolated between the lines of a hymn as a mass response to a leader's singing of a line; often containing ejaculations ("shouting words").

Minorizing: changing a modal tune into a minor one by adding accidentals.

Modes: a "selection of tones arranged in a scale, that form the basic substance of a composition." (Definition adapted from *Harvard Dictionary of Music.*) The modes in common use in campmeeting spirituals are:

Major:	CDEFGABC
Minor:	ABCDEF(or F#)G#A
Dorian:	DEFGABCD
Mixolydian:	GABCDEFG
Aeolian:	ABCDEFGA (natural minor)

(These patterns may be transposed to any key.)

Mother-hymn: the words of a "standard" hymn, in part or whole (usually set to a folk-hymn tune), to which has been attached a campmeeting chorus.

Refrain: a very brief repeated section of a song.

Revival meetings: evangelistic meetings started in America in the first half of the eighteenth century ("First Great Awakening"), strong again at the end of that century and beginning of the nineteenth ("Second Great Awakening"), and continuing with peaks in the 1820s and late 1850s, especially in the urban areas of the Northeast.

Revival songs or *revival spirituals:* same as campmeeting songs. The songs taking form at country camp meetings were also sung at urban revival meetings.

Sequence: a melodic pattern repeated on different degrees of the scale.

Song: an informal hymn, often with a chorus.

Songbook: a book of informal sacred songs or hymns.

Songster: a small book of hymn-texts, most campmeeting-related.

Spiritual: originally "spiritual song" (see Ephesians 5:19) with the connotation of an individual rather than a corporate act of praise.

Tunebook: an eighteenth- and nineteenth-century type of hymnal distinguished by its oblong shape, its presentation of tunes as well as at least one stanza of text, and (usually) its introductory lessons in musical theory and/or singing.

Western air: a hymn tune coming from the frontier camp meetings. (The term was used in the hymnals and songbooks of the nineteenth century.)

Western frontier: 1790s, Kentucky and Tennessee; from 1800 on, the states north of the Ohio River, then gradually Michigan, Missouri, Iowa, Wisconsin, and the Deep South.

Notes and References

Preface
1. George Pullen Jackson, *Spiritual Folk Songs of Early America* (New York: J. J. Augustin, 1937; reprinted by Dover Publications, New York, 1964), p. 23.

Part I. Camp Meetings: How They Began
1. George Pullen Jackson, *Another Sheaf of White Spirituals* (Gainesville: University of Florida Press, 1952), p. 285.
2. Don Yoder, *Pennsylvania Spirituals* (Lancaster: Pennsylvania Folklife Society, 1961), p. 449.
3. The dates of admission to statehood give a good guide to the development of the frontier: Kentucky, 1792; Tennessee, 1796; Ohio, 1803; Mississippi, 1817; Illinois, 1818; Indiana, 1819; Alabama, 1819; Missouri, 1821.
4. The First Great Awakening began with the magnetic preaching of Jonathan Edwards in New England and the stirring revivals of the English preacher George Whitefield. The spirit flowed with the Baptists and Presbyterians to the South, and was instrumental in the success of the Methodist movement organized in 1784.
5. A. McLean and J. W. Eaton, *Penuel, or Face to Face with God* (New York: W. C. Palmer, Jr., Publisher, 1869), p. 466. "At the consecration of the elements, a sacramental hymn was sung with melting emotion."
6. Tobias Spicer, *Camp Meetings Defended* (New Haven: T. G. Woodward, 1828), pp. 22, 23.
7. A. P. Mead, *Manna in the Wilderness,* 3rd ed. (Philadelphia: Perkenpine & Higgins, 1860), p. 85.
8. Francis Ward, *Minutes of a Camp Meeting Held by the Methodists in the Town of Carmel, Dutchess Co., 1804* (New York: John C. Totten, 1804), p. 10. (Pamphlet.)
9. Mead, *Manna,* p. 240.
10. John Fetterhof, *Life of John Fetterhof of the United Brethren in Christ* (Chambersburg, Pa.: United Brethren in Christ Print, 1883), p. 191.
11. G. W. Henry, *Trials and Triumphs in the Life of G. W. Henry* (Oneida: G. W. Henry, 1853, 1856), p. 269.
12. *A Narrative of the Revival of Religion in the County of Oneida* (Utica: Hastings and Tracy, 1826), p. 11.

13. L. C. Rudolph, *Francis Asbury* (Nashville: Abingdon, 1966), p. 120.
14. Preface to *Hallowed Songs*, 1866.
15. E. S. Lorenz, Preface to *Church Hymnal*, 1935.
16. See Part V for illustrative campmeeting spirituals.
17. James B. Finley, *Autobiography; or, Pioneer Life in the West*, ed. W. P. Strickland (Cincinnati: Methodist Book Concern, 1854), p. 345.
18. Mead, *Manna*, p. 126.
19. E. S. Lorenz, *Practical Church Music* (New York: Fleming H. Revell Company, 1909), p. 93.
20. Mead, *Manna*, p. 200.
21. Finley, *Autobiography*, p. 315.
22. Charles C. Cole, Jr., *The Social Ideas of the Northern Evangelists. Columbia Studies in the Social Sciences*, No. 580 (New York: Columbia University Press, 1954), p. 74.
23. Peter Cartwright, *Autobiography of Peter Cartwright, the Backwoods Preacher* (Cincinnati: Cranston and Curts, n.d. [1856?]), p. 312.
24. *Ibid.*, p. 476.
25. Especially interesting to me is Fetterhof's long and affectionate friendship with my great-great-grandfather, Bishop Henry Kumler, Jr., Fetterhof's mentor and frequent companion in travel.
26. Fetterhof, *Life of John Fetterhof*, pp. 170, 204.
27. Dickson D. Bruce, *And They All Sang Hallelujah: Plain-Folk Campmeeting Religion, 1800–1845* (Knoxville: University of Tennessee Press, 1974), p. 75.
28. Whitney R. Cross, *The Burned-Over District: the Social and Intellectual History of Enthusiastic Religion in Western New York, 1800–1850* (Ithaca: Cornell University Press, 1950), p. 101.
29. *Ibid.*, pp. 14, 15.
30. *Ibid.*, p. 275.
31. Cole, *The Social Ideas of the Northern Evangelists*, p. 96.
32. Warren A. Candler, *Great Revivals and the Great Republic* (Nashville: Publishing House of the Methodist Episcopal Church South, 1904), p. 191.
33. Henry C. Fish, *Handbook of Revivals* (Boston: James H. Earle, 1874), p. 317.
34. Ephraim Perkins, *A "Bunker Hill" Contest* (Utica: H. and E. Phinney, 1826). (Pamphlet.)
35. Cross, *The Burned-Over District*, pp. 173, 174.
36. "No political party in American history has championed a doctrine so utterly leveling" (*ibid.*, p. 271). "Christian enthusiasts through the ages had anticipated an early millennium: a thousand years of heaven on earth which were to precede Christ's Second Coming, the day of judgment, and the end of the world. . . . Probably well over fifty thousand people in the United States became convinced that time would run out in 1844." (*Ibid.*, p. 287.)
37. Cole, *The Social Ideas of the Northern Evangelists*, pp. 92, 94.
38. Among the approximately 250 revival songbooks examined in this study, no fewer than 42 were issued by one denomination—the Methodists—between 1811 and 1875.

NOTES AND REFERENCES

Part II. Campmeeting Spirituals: How They Happened

1. Watts, *Alas, and did my Savior bleed;* Doddridge, *O happy day that fixed my choice;* Wesley, *Come, sinners, to the gospel feast;* Hart, *Come, ye sinners poor and needy;* Stennett, *On Jordan's stormy banks I stand;* Medley, *I know that my Redeemer lives,* and so on.
2. "Hymnal," though the proper term for a book containing words and tunes, is too formal for a book containing campmeeting songs.
3. William Warren Sweet, in his *Religion in the Development of American Culture, 1765–1840* (New York: Scribner's, 1952), p. 154, says: "Both Baptists and Methodists produced religious songs which grew out of the crude frontier conditions and which may properly be classed as folk songs. The Presbyterians and Congregationalists were psalm singers, and their singing was not so important to them as to Methodists and Baptists."
4. See Enoch Mudge's naïvely charming hymns describing phases of the campmeeting experience in his songster, *The American Campmeeting Hymnbook,* 1818.
5. David Klocko, in his studies of folk tunes in western New England at the turn of the nineteenth century, has found the secular sources for several dozen tunes first appearing in print in *Christian Harmony,* 1805; and documents them in his unpublished Ph.D. dissertation, "Jeremiah Ingalls's *The Christian Harmony; or, Songster's Companion* (1805)," University of Michigan, 1978.
6. George Pullen Jackson, *Down-East Spirituals and Others* (Locust Valley, N.Y.: J. J. Augustin, Publisher, n.d. [1942?]), pp. 3, 4.
7. B. St. James Fry, "The Early Camp Meeting Song Writers," *The Methodist (Quarterly) Review,* Vol. XI (July, 1859), p. 407.
8. Lorenz, *Practical Church Music,* p. 91.
9. Louis F. Benson, *The English Hymn: Its Development and Use in Worship* (New York: Hodder & Stoughton; George Doran Company, 1915), p. 285.
10. William R. Phinney, *Prattsville District Camp Meetings* (Prattsville, N.Y., n.d. [Typescript]).
11. Lorenz, *Practical Church Music,* p. 92.
12. Fry, "The Early Camp Meeting Song Writers," p. 407.
13. George Pullen Jackson, *White Spirituals of the Southern Uplands* (Chapel Hill: University of North Carolina Press, 1933; reprinted by Folklore Associates, Hatboro, Pa., 1964), p. 237.
14. Jackson, *Another Sheaf of White Spirituals,* p. xi.
15. Charles A. Johnson, *The Frontier Camp Meeting* (Dallas: Southern Methodist University Press, 1955), p. 134.
16. John B. Boles, *The Great Revival, 1787–1805: The Origins of the Southern Evangelical Mind* (Lexington: University Press of Kentucky, 1972), p. 121.
17. Johnson, *The Frontier Camp Meeting,* p. 207.
18. McLean and Eaton, *Penuel,* p. 393.
19. Benson, *The English Hymn,* p. 276.
20. See Yoder's *Pennsylvania Spirituals.*
21. Hazel Spencer Phillips, *Richard the Shaker* (Lebanon, Ohio: By the Author, 1972), p. 49.

135

22. Edward D. Andrews, *The Gift to Be Simple* (New York: J. J. Augustin, 1940), p. 112.
23. Austin C. Caswell, "Social and Moral Music: The Hymn," *Music in American Society 1776–1976,* ed. George McCue (New Brunswick, N.J.: Transaction Books, 1977), p. 70.
24. George Pullen Jackson, *White and Negro Spirituals* (New York: J. J. Augustin, 1944; reprinted by DaCapo Press, New York, 1975), p. 83.
25. L. L. McDowell, *Songs of the Old Camp Ground* (Ann Arbor: Edwards Brothers, Inc., 1937), p. 30.
26. Lorenz, *Practical Church Music,* pp. 93, 94.
27. Fry, "The Early Camp Meeting Song Writers," p. 408.
28. See my essay, "The Devil's Good Tunes: The Secular in Protestant Hymnody," unpublished portion of M.S.M. thesis, Wittenberg University, 1971, reprinted in part in *The Diapason,* January, 1972, pp. 18-20. The essay endeavors to show that secular music has been used at all times of great surging religious activity, including the present.
29. *Harvard Dictionary of Music,* 2nd ed., 1969, p. 542.
30. William Chappell, *Popular Music of the Olden Time* (London: Chappell and Co., 1859; reprinted by Dover Publications, New York, 1965), p. 748.
31. See George Pullen Jackson, "Stephen Foster's Debt to American Folk Song," *The Musical Quarterly,* April, 1936, pp. 154-69; and E. S. Lorenz, *Practical Church Music,* p. 92.
32. Sigmund Spaeth, *A History of Popular Music in America* (New York: Random House, 1948), pp. 147-48.
33. Jackson, *Down-East Spirituals,* p. 239.
34. James Weldon Johnson and J. Rosamond Johnson, *The Books of American Negro Spirituals* (New York: Viking Press, 1925, 1926), p. 20.
35. William Francis Allen, Charles Pickard Ware, and Lucy McKim Garrison, *Slave Songs in the United States* (New York: Peter Smith, 1951 [1867]), p. ix.
36. See Jackson, *White and Negro Spirituals,* chap. XXI.
37. Newman Ivey White, *American Negro Folk-Songs* (Hatboro, Pa.: Folklore Associates, 1965; facsimile of the original edition, Harvard University Press, 1928), p. 49.
38. Miles Mark Fisher, *Negro Slave Songs in the United States* (New York: Russell & Russell, 1968), p. 15.
39. John W. Work, *American Negro Songs* (New York: Howell, Soskin & Co., 1940), p. 12.
40. Dena J. Epstein, *Sinful Tunes and Spirituals* (Urbana: University of Illinois Press, 1977), p. 199.
41. Albert Buffington, *Dutchified German Spirituals,* vol. 62 (Lancaster, Pa.: Pennsylvania German Society, 1965).

Part III. Campmeeting Spirituals Come into Print
1. David Klocko, letter to the present writer, September 22, 1977.
2. William Jensen Reynolds, *Hymns of Our Faith: a Handbook for the Baptist Hymnal* (Nashville: Broadman Press, 1964), p. xxii.

NOTES AND REFERENCES

3. Jackson, *White and Negro Spirituals,* p. 71.
4. Irving Lowens, *Music and Musicians in Early America* (New York: W. W. Norton, 1964), pp. 138-39.
5. Irving Lowens, Preface to Wyeth's *Repository of Sacred Music, Part Second* (Reprint of 2nd ed. [1820] by DaCapo Press, New York, 1964), p. vii.
6. Frederick A. Norwood, *The Story of American Methodism* (Nashville: Abingdon, 1974), p. 232.
7. For a detailed study of *The Revivalist,* see Ellen Jane Lorenz Porter's Ph.D. dissertation, *A Treasure of Campmeeting Spirituals,* Microfilms International, Ann Arbor, Michigan (No. 79-16,965).
8. Jackson, *White and Negro Spirituals,* p. 104.
9. Leonard Ellinwood, "Religious Music in America," *The Religious Perspective in American Culture,* vol. II, ed. James Ward Smith and A. Leland Jamison (Princeton: Princeton University Press, 1961), p. 324.
10. F. P. Jones, *American Methodist Tune Books 1807–1878* (Evanston: Garrett Biblical Institute, n.d. [Typescript]), p. 128.
11. Cole, *The Social Ideas of the Northern Evangelists,* p. 57.

Part IV. The Persistence of the Spirit of the Camp Meetings and Their Songs

1. From *Charles E. Ives: Memos,* ed. John Kirkpatrick (W. W. Norton, 1972), not paged.
2. "Back to That Old-Time Religion," *Time,* December 26, 1977, pp. 52-57.
3. Nathan L. Gerrard, "The Holiness Movement in Southern Appalachia," *The Charismatic Movement,* ed. Michael Hamilton (Grand Rapids: Eerdmans, 1975), p. 167.
4. Eleanor Dickinson and Barbara Benziger, *Revival!* (New York: Harper & Row, 1974), p. 167.
5. H. L. Mencken, "The Hills of Zion," in *The American Scene* (New York: Alfred A. Knopf, 1965), pp. 261-65.
6. Marjorie Hyer, "Charismatics Held Baptism Lessons," *Dayton Journal-Herald,* July 30, 1977, p. 16.
7. *Music in Catholic Worship* (Washington: United States Catholic Conference, 1972), pp. 5, 13, and 19.
8. *Monthly Missalette* (Chicago: J. S. Paluch Company), Vol. 12, No. 10 (December, 1976), and Vol. 13, No. 1 (1977).
9. For an analysis of the content of a number of such collections and programs, see "The Devil's Good Tunes," *The Diapason,* January, 1972, p. 20.
10. *Genesis* (Carol Stream, Ill.: Agape, 1973).
11. Joel Rosenman, Jon Roberts, and Robert Pilpel, *Young Men with Unlimited Capital* (New York: Harcourt Brace Jovanovich, 1974), p. 153.

Part V. Song Examples

1. E. S. Lorenz, *Practical Church Music,* p. 100.
2. Jackson, *Spiritual Folk Songs of Early America,* p. 171.

3. Allen, Ware, and Garrison, *Slave Songs of the United States,* p. 8.
4. Yoder, *Pennsylvania Spirituals,* pp. 346, 407.
5. Jackson, *White Spirituals in the Southern Uplands,* p. 149.
6. David Klocko, in a letter to me.
7. Gilbert Chase, *America's Music from the Pilgrims to the Present,* rev. 2nd ed. (New York: McGraw Hill, 1966), p. 214.
8. Jackson, *Spiritual Folk Songs of Early America,* p. 238.
9. Jackson, *White Spirituals in the Southern Uplands,* p. 139.
10. Yoder, *Pennsylvania Spirituals,* p. 161.
11. L. A. Banks, *Immortal Songs of Camp and Field* (Cleveland: Burrows, 1898), p. 97.
12. Andrews, *The Gift to Be Simple,* p. 112.
13. H. Wiley Hitchcock, *Music in the United States: A Historical Introduction* (Englewood Cliffs, N.J.: Prentice-Hall, 1969), p. 97.
14. Yoder, *Pennsylvania Spirituals,* p. 411.
15. Charles W. Ferguson, *Organizing to Beat the Devil: Methodists and the Making of America* (Garden City, N.Y.: Doubleday, 1971), p. 90.

Recommended Reading: A Short Bibliography

(For authors of works quoted in this book, see the Index of Persons and Songbooks. Bibliographical references are listed in Notes and References. The asterisks indicate especially helpful items.)

*Allen, William Francis; Ware, Charles Pickard; and Garrison, Lucy McKim. *Slave Songs in the United States*. New York: Peter Smith, 1951 (1867). (With music.)

Asbury, Francis. *The Journals and Letters of Francis Asbury*. Vol. II. Ed. Elmer T. Clark. Nashville: Abingdon Press, 1958.

*Benson, Louis F. *The English Hymn: Its Development and Use in Worship*. New York: Hodder & Stoughton; George Doran Company, 1915.

*Boles, John B. *The Great Revival, 1787–1805: The Origins of the Southern Evangelical Mind*. Lexington: University Press of Kentucky, 1972. Chapter 8.

*Bruce, Dickson D., Jr. *And They All Sang Hallelujah: Plain-Folk Camp-meeting Religion, 1800–1845*. Knoxville: University of Tennessee Press, 1974.

*Cartwright, Peter. *Autobiography of Peter Cartwright, the Backwoods Preacher*. Cincinnati: Cranston and Curts, n.d. (1856?).

Caswell, Austin C. "Social and Moral Music: The Hymn." *Music in American Society 1776–1976*. Ed. George McCue. New Brunswick, N.J.: Transaction Books, 1977.

Chase, Gilbert. *America's Music from the Pilgrims to the Present*. Rev. 2nd ed. New York: McGraw Hill, 1955, 1966. Chapter 11. (With music.)

*Cleveland, Catherine C. *The Great Revival in the West*. Chicago: University of Chicago Press, 1916.

*Cole, Charles C., Jr. *The Social Ideas of the Northern Evangelists*. *Columbia Studies in the Social Sciences*, No. 580. New York: Columbia University Press, 1954.

Courlander, Harold. *Negro Folk Music in the U.S.A.* New York: Columbia University Press, 1963. (With music.)

*Cross, Whitney R. *The Burned-Over District: The Social and Intellectual History of Enthusiastic Religion in Western New York, 1800–1850*. Ithaca: Cornell University Press, 1950.

Dickinson, Eleanor, and Benziger, Barbara. *Revival!* New York: Harper & Row, 1974.

GLORY, HALLELUJAH!

*Ellinwood, Leonard. "Religious Music in America." *The Religious Perspective in American Culture*, II, 289-359. James Ward Smith and A. Leland Jamison, eds. Princeton: Princeton University Press, 1961.
*Epstein, Dena J. *Sinful Tunes and Spirituals.* Urbana: University of Illinois Press, 1977.
———. "Slave Music in the United States Before 1860: A Survey of Sources." *Notes of the Music Library Association,* Vol. 20, Spring, 1963, pp. 195-212, 377-90.
Ferguson, Charles W. *Organizing to Beat the Devil: Methodists and the Making of America.* Garden City, N.Y.: Doubleday, 1971.
*Fetterhof, John. *Life of John Fetterhof of the United Brethren in Christ.* Chambersburg, Pa.: United Brethren in Christ Print, 1883.
*Finley, James B. *Autobiography: or, Pioneer Life in the West.* W. P. Strickland, ed. Cincinnati: Methodist Book Concern, 1854.
*Fisher, Miles Mark. *Negro Slave Songs in the United States.* New York: Russell & Russell, 1968.
*Fry, B. St. James. "The Early Camp Meeting Song Writers." *The Methodist (Quarterly) Review,* Vol. XI, July, 1859, pp. 401-13.
Gewehr, W. M. "Some Factors in the Expansion of Frontier Methodism, 1800–1811." *Journal of Religion*, Vol. VIII, January, 1928, pp. 98-120.
Henry, G. W. *Trials and Triumphs in the Life of G. W. Henry.* Oneida: G. W. Henry, 1853, 1856.
Hitchcock, H. Wiley. *Music in the United States: A Historical Introduction.* Englewood Cliffs, N. J.: Prentice-Hall, 1969.
*Jackson, George Pullen. *Another Sheaf of White Spirituals.* Gainesville: University of Florida Press, 1952. (With music.)
*———. *Down-East Spirituals and Others.* Locust Valley, N.Y.: J. J. Augustin, Publisher, n.d. (1942?). (With music.)
*———. *Spiritual Folk Songs of Early America.* New York: J. J. Augustin, Publisher, 1937. Reprinted by Dover Publications, New York, 1964. (With music.)
*———. *White and Negro Spirituals.* New York: J. J. Augustin, 1944. Reprinted by DaCapo Press, New York, 1975. (With music.)
*———. *White Spirituals of the Southern Uplands.* Chapel Hill: University of North Carolina Press, 1933. Reprinted by Folklore Associates, Hatboro, Pa., 1964. (With music.)
*Johnson, Charles A. *The Frontier Camp Meeting.* Dallas: Southern Methodist University Press, 1955.
Johnson, James Weldon, and Johnson, J. Rosamond. *The Books of American Negro Spirituals.* New York: Viking Press, 1925, 1926. (With music.)
*Klocko, David G. "Jeremiah Ingalls's *The Christian Harmony; or, Songster's Companion* (1805)." Unpublished Ph.D. dissertation, University of Michigan, 1978.
*Lorenz, E. S. *Practical Church Music.* New York: Fleming H. Revell Company, 1909. (With a few campmeeting songs.)
Lowens, Irving. *Music and Musicians in Early America.* New York: W. W. Norton, 1964.
*McDowell, L. L. *Songs of the Old Camp Ground.* Ann Arbor: Edwards Brothers, 1937. (With music.)

BIBLIOGRAPHY

McLoughlin, William G., Jr. *Modern Revivalism: Charles Grandison Finney to Billy Graham.* New York: The Ronald Press Company, 1959.

McNemar, Richard. *The Kentucky Revival, or, a Short History of the Late Extraordinary Outpouring of the Spirit of God in the Western States of America.* Cincinnati, 1807. Reprinted by E. O. Jenkins, New York, 1846.

Mead, A. P. *Manna in the Wilderness.* 3rd ed. Philadelphia: Perkenpine & Higgins, 1860.

Metcalf, Frank J. *American Writers and Compilers of Sacred Music.* New York: Russell & Russell, 1925.

Phillips, Hazel Spencer. *Richard the Shaker.* Lebanon, Ohio: Published by the author, 1972.

Porter, Ellen J. Lorenz. "The Devil's Good Tunes: The Secular in Protestant Hymnody." Part of requirements for the M.S.M. degree, Wittenberg University, 1971. Reprinted in part in *The Diapason,* January, 1972.

*Rudolph, L. C. *Francis Asbury.* Nashville: Abingdon, 1966.

*Seldes, Gilbert. *The Stammering Century.* New York: The John Day Company, 1927, 1928.

Norwood, Frederick A. *The Story of American Methodism.* Nashville: Abingdon, 1974.

Sweet, William Warren. *Circuit-Rider Days Along the Ohio.* New York: The Methodist Book Concern, 1923.

*———. *Religion in the Development of American Culture, 1765–1840.* New York: Charles Scribner's Sons, 1952.

———. *Religion on the American Frontier.* Vol. IV, *The Methodists.* Chicago: University of Chicago Press, 1946.

———. *Revivalism in America.* New York: Charles Scribner's Sons, 1945.

———. *The Rise of Methodism in the West.* Nashville: The Methodist Book Concern, 1920.

Watters, Philip M. *Peter Cartwright.* New York: Eaton & Mains, 1910.

*Weisberger, Bernard A. *They Gathered at the River.* Boston: Little, Brown, 1958.

*White, Newman Ivey. *American Negro Folk-Songs.* Hatboro, Pa.: Folklore Associates, 1965 (facsimile of the original edition, Harvard University Press, 1928).

Woodward, William W. *Surprising Accounts of the Revival of Religion.* Philadelphia: William Woodward, 1802.

Work, John W. *American Negro Songs.* New York: Howell, Soskin & Co., 1940. (With music.)

*Yoder, Don. *Pennsylvania Spirituals.* Lancaster: Pennsylvania Folklife Society, 1961. (With music.)

*Young, Jacob. *Autobiography of a Pioneer.* Cincinnati: L. Swormstedt and Poe, for the Methodist Episcopal Church, 1859.

Index
of Persons and Songbooks

Items in footnotes, and titles of songbooks, are in italic type. In case of multiple authorship, only the first author is listed here.

142

INDEX

Finley, James B., 15, 27, 31, 134
Finney, Charles Grandison, 34-36
Fish, Henry C., 134
Fisher, Miles Mark, 65, 136
Foster, Stephen, 62, 136
Fry, B., St. James, 30, 42, 61, 135-36

Gealy, Fred D., 48
Genesis, 85, 137
Gerrard, Nathan, 137
Gewehr, W. M., 47
Gift to Be Simple, The, 138
Good Old Songs, 68-69
Gorham, B. W., 60, 118
Granade, John, 60-61

Hallowed Songs, 74, 99, 103, 134
Hammond, Edward P., 35, 38
Hart, Joseph, 16, 53, 135
Hauser, William, 61
Henry, G. W., 31, 133
Hillman, Joseph, 10, 36-37
Hinde, Thomas S., 60
Hitchcock, H. Wiley, 138
Howe, Julia Ward, 63
Hutchinson Family, 93
Hyer, Marjorie, 137
Hymns for the Sanctuary, 9, 76

Ingalls, Jeremiah, 71, 91, 135
Ives, Charles, 82, 137

Jackson, George Pullen, 10-11, 42, 50, 52, 71, 87, 107, 133, 135-38
Johnson, Charles A., 135
Johnson, James Weldon, 64, 136
Jones, F. P., 137
Jones, Edmund, 53
Jubilee Harp, 75, 93, 126

Kentucky Harmony, 72, 74
Klocko, David, 71, 135-36, 138
Knapp, Jacob, 74

Leavitt, Jonathan, 72
Lee, Luther, 38
Lewis, Freeman, 61

Lincoln, Abraham, 24
Lorenz, E. S., 9-12, 43-44, 51, 59, 87, 134-37
Lowens, Irving, 72, 137
Lute of Zion, The, 74, 113, 114
Luther, Martin, 62

McDowell, L. L., 136
McGready, James, 16
McLean, A., 30, 133, 135
McNemar, Richard, 31, 45
Maffitt, John, 36
Mason, Lowell, 69
Mead, A. P., 26, 28, 133-34
Medley, Samuel, 48, 135
Mencken, H. L., 83, 137
Methodist Hymnal (1966), 48, 74
Millennial Harp, 75, 93
Miller, William, 75
Mills, Elizabeth, 53
Monthly Missalette, 84, 137
Mudge, Enoch, 26, 135

Nettleton, Asahel, 36
Nevin, John W., 32
New Jubilee Harp, 76
New Song, The, 74, 101, 102
Norwood, Frederick A., 137

Olive Leaf, The, 61, 75
Otterbein Hymnal, 76

Parker, Orson, 39
Pentecostal Hymns No. 1, 119
Perkins, Ephraim, 134
Phillips, Hazel Spencer, 135
Phinney, William R., 135
Pilgrim's Songster, 60
Plummer, Frederick, 33
Plymouth Collection, 46, 76
Practical Church Music, 10, 87, 135-36
Prayer Meeting Hymn Book 77
Primitive Baptist Hymnal, 90
Primitive Baptist Hymn and Tune Book, 74
Psalmodist's Companion, The, 90

Rankin, Adam, 29, 33
Repository of Sacred Music, Part Second, 72, 74, 92

GLORY, HALLELUJAH!